Learn Swift 2 on the Mac

Second Edition

Waqar Malik

Apress®

Learn Swift 2 on the Mac, Second Edition

ISBN-13 (pbk): 978-1-4842-1628-6

ISBN-13 (electronic): 978-1-4842-1627-9

Managing Director: Welmoed Spahr
Lead Editor: Michelle Lowman
Technical Reviewer: Felipe Laso Marsetti
Editorial Board: Steve Anglin, Pramila Balan, Louise Corrigan, James T. DeWolf, Jonathan Gennick, Robert Hutchinson, Celestin Suresh John, Michelle Lowman, James Markham, Susan McDermott, Matthew Moodie, Jeffrey Pepper, Douglas Pundick, Ben Renow-Clarke, Gwenan Spearing
Coordinating Editor: Mark Powers
Copy Editor: Karen Jameson
Compositor: SPi Global
Indexer: SPi Global
Artist: SPi Global

Distributed to the book trade worldwide by Springer Science+Business Media New York, 233 Spring Street, 6th Floor, New York, NY 10013. Phone 1-800-SPRINGER, fax (201) 348-4505, e-mail `orders-ny@springer-sbm.com`, or visit `www.springeronline.com`. Apress Media, LLC is a California LLC and the sole member (owner) is Springer Science + Business Media Finance Inc (SSBM Finance Inc). SSBM Finance Inc is a Delaware corporation.

For information on translations, please e-mail `rights@apress.com`, or visit `www.apress.com`.

Apress and friends of ED books may be purchased in bulk for academic, corporate, or promotional use. eBook versions and licenses are also available for most titles. For more information, reference our Special Bulk Sales–eBook Licensing web page at `www.apress.com/bulk-sales`.

Any source code or other supplementary materials referenced by the author in this text is available to readers at `www.apress.com/9781484216286`. For detailed information about how to locate your book's source code, go to `www.apress.com/source-code/`. Readers can also access source code at SpringerLink in the Supplementary Material section for each chapter.

For my family, Irrum, Mishal, and Adam.

Contents at a Glance

Contents

About the Author

Waqar Malik worked at Apple helping developers write Cocoa applications for the Mac during the early days of Mac OS X. Now he develops applications for various Apple OS platforms. He is the co-author of *Learn Objective-C on the Mac* (Apress, 2012).

About the Technical Reviewer

Felipe Laso Marsetti is an iOS programmer working at Lextech Global Services. He loves everything related to Apple, video games, cooking, and playing the violin, piano, or guitar. In his spare time, Felipe loves to read and learn new programming languages or technologies.

Felipe likes to write on his blog at `http://iFe.li`, create iOS tutorials and articles as a member of `www.raywenderlich.com`, and work as a technical reviewer for Objective-C and iOS–related books. You can find him on Twitter as `@Airjordan12345`, on Facebook under his name, or on `App.net` as `@iFeli`.

Acknowledgments

I'd like to give thanks to all the folks at Apress who helped complete this book. This book would not have been possible without their assistance.

Introduction

Whenever developers come to a new platform, they are faced with the task of getting to know unfamiliar development tools, design patterns, the standard frameworks available in the new environment, and perhaps even a new programming language.

Most of the time, this is all done while trying to deliver an application as soon as possible. In such situations, developers tend to fall back on the patterns and approaches they are familiar with from previous environments, which too often results in code that doesn't fit the new environment, or in duplicate code that might already be provided by the built-in frameworks. This can cause problems down the road or delays in delivery.

It would be great to have colleagues already familiar with the platform who could offer guidance to get you going in the right direction. Well, it's not always possible to have mentors to help you, and that's where this books steps in—to be your mentor.

The author of this book is a veteran of Apple's Developer Technical Services organization, and has answered countless questions from software engineers who are new to Apple technology. That experience results in a book that anticipates the most common misunderstandings and takes care to explain not only the how, but also the why of Apple's development platform.

Learn Swift 2 on the Mac provides a step-by-step guide that will help you acquire the skills you need to develop applications for OS X, iOS, watchOS, and tvOS.

Chapter 1

Hello Swift

Swift is a new language designed by Apple for developing iOS and OS X applications. It takes the best parts of C and Objective-C and adapts them with modern features and patterns. Swift-compiled programs will run on iOS7 or newer and OS X 10.9 (Mavericks) or newer.

The two main goals for the language are compatibility with the Cocoa and Cocoa Touch frameworks and safety, as you'll see in the upcoming chapters. If you've been using Objective-C, especially the modern syntax, Swift will feel familiar.

However, Swift's syntax is actually a major departure from Objective-C. It takes lots of cues from programming languages such as Haskell, C#, Ruby, and Python.

Some of the technologies we will cover in this book are the following:

- Automatic reference counting
- Closures (blocks)
- Collection literals
- Modules
- Frameworks
- Objective-C runtime
- Generics
- Operator overloading
- Tuples
- Namespaces
- Error Handling

Improvements over Objective-C

Let's take a quick look at some of the features that make Swift better than Objective-C. We will cover these topics in detail in later chapters.

Type Inference

One of the key features of Swift is type inference. But what is type inference? It means that you can figure out the type of the variable by the value it is assigned. There is usually no need to specify the type of variables (though you can always specify them); the types of the variables can be inferred by the value being set.

Type Safety

Swift variables must have a type and must be initialized before they can be used. Conversion between different types is done explicitly; you cannot simply assign a float to an integer.

```
let floatValue : Float = 4.0
let doubleValue : Double = floatValue // This is an error
```

There is not automatic conversion even though Double can hold the value that float holds. To correctly convert, we need to create a new value of type before assigning:

```
let doubleValue : Double = Double(floatValue)
```

Swift compiler knows more about types in method calls and uses table look-up for method dispatch instead of the dynamic dispatch that is used by Objective-C. Static method dispatch via table look-up enables more checks and validation at compile time, even in the playground. As soon as you enter an expression in the playground, the compiler evaluates it and lets you know of any possible issues with the statement; you can't run your program until you fix those issues. Here are some features that enhance safety:

- Variables and constants are always initialized before use.
- Array bounds are always checked.
- Raw C pointers are not readily available and are discouraged.
- Assignment statements do not return values.
- Overflows are trapped as runtime errors.

Control Flow

The switch statement has undergone a major overhaul. Now it can select based not only integers, but also on strings, floats, and ranges of items, expressions, enums, and so forth. Moreover, there's no implicit fall-through between case statements.

Also introduced a *guard* statement. A guard statement is like an if statement but with an additional requirement of always having an `else` statement.

Optionals

Variable values can be optional. What does that mean? It means that a variable will either be nil or it will have a valid value. The nil value is distinct from any valid value. Optionals can also be chained together to protect against errors and exceptions.

Strings

Strings in Swift are much easier to work with; they have a clear, simple syntax. You can concatenate strings using the += operator. The mutability of the strings is defined by the language, not the `String` object. You declare a string as either mutable or nonmutable with the same `String` object, by using either the `let` or `var` keywords.

Unicode

Unicode is supported at the core: You can define variable names and function names using full Unicode. The `String` and `Character` types are also fully Unicode compliant and support various encodings, such as UTF-8, UTF-16, and 21-bit Unicode scalers.

Other Improvements

- Header files are no longer required.
- Functions are full-fledged objects; they can be passed as arguments and returned from other functions. Functions can be scoped similarly to instance variables.
- Comments can be nested.
- There are separate operators for assignment (=) and comparison (==), and there's even an identity operator (===) for checking whether two data elements refer to the same object.
- There is no defined entry point for programs such as main.

If all this sounds good to you (it does to me), let's go get the tools to start playing with Swift.

Requirements

Before you can begin playing with Swift, you need to download and install Xcode, the IDE that's used to build applications for iOS and OS X. You'll need Xcode 7.1 or later.

It's really easy to download and install Xcode. Here are the basic requirements:

- Intel-based Macintosh computer
- OS X 10.11 El Capitan (or later)
- 15GB of free disk space
- An Internet connection to download Xcode and documentation
- An iOS device running iOS 9 (or later)

> **Note** As a rule, the later the version of the OS, the better. The examples in the book are developed using Xcode 7.1 running on OS X 10.11 El Capitan and for iOS 9.1 running on iPhone 6s.

Getting Xcode

Launch the App Store application and use the search bar on the top right to search for Xcode. You can then get more information by selecting Xcode, as shown in Figure 1-1, or install it by selecting the Install button.

***Figure 1-1.** Xcode on App Store*

When you launch Xcode for the first time, it will download and install other required items in order to complete the installation. If you have multiple versions of Xcode installed, be sure to select Xcode version 7 or later for the command-line tools. You can do this by selecting **Xcode ➤ Preferences**, then choosing the **Locations** tab as shown in Figure 1-2.

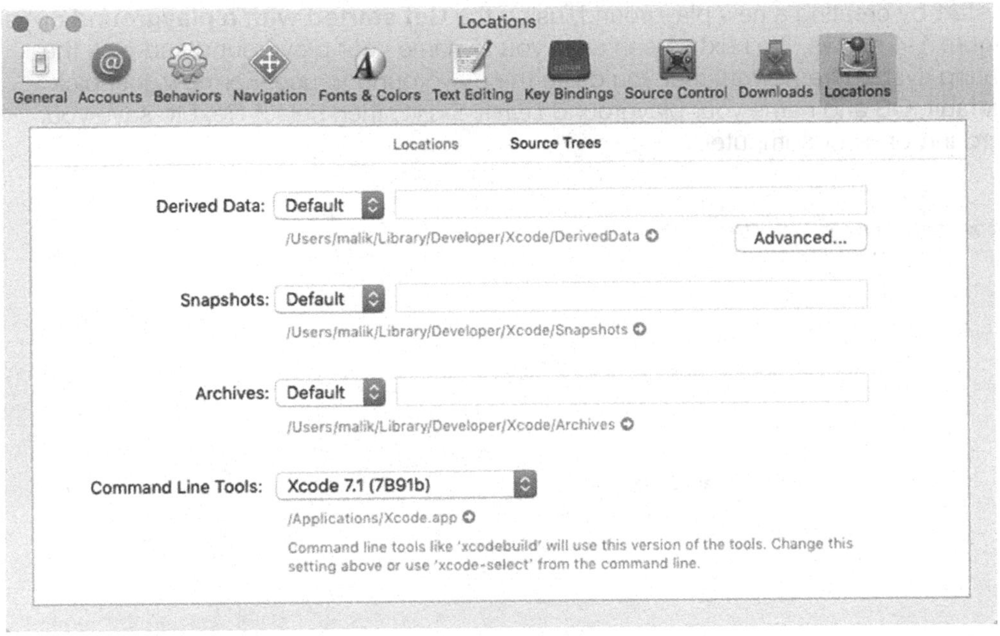

Figure 1-2. Selecting the command-line tools

Quick Tour of Xcode

If you launch Xcode without opening a project, you'll see the screen shown in Figure 1-3. You can create or open existing projects or a playground.

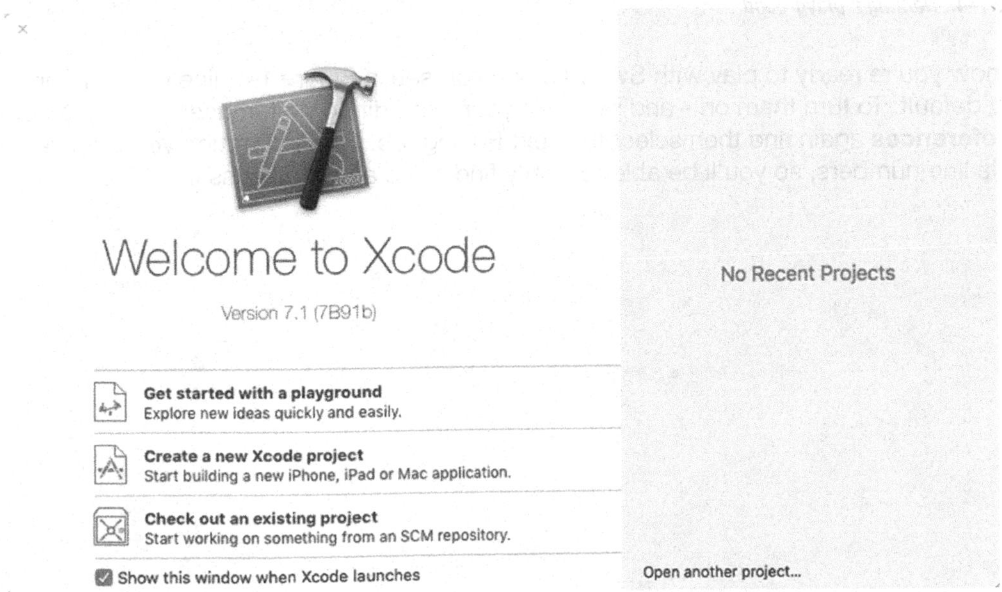

Figure 1-3. Xcode Welcome Screen

Let's start by creating a new playground, using the **Get started with a playground** option. As Figure 1-4 shows, the next screen asks you to name your playground and pick the operating system framework that you'd like the playground to use. For now, just pick the default iOS and name your playground `Learn Swift`, then select Next to save your playground on your computer.

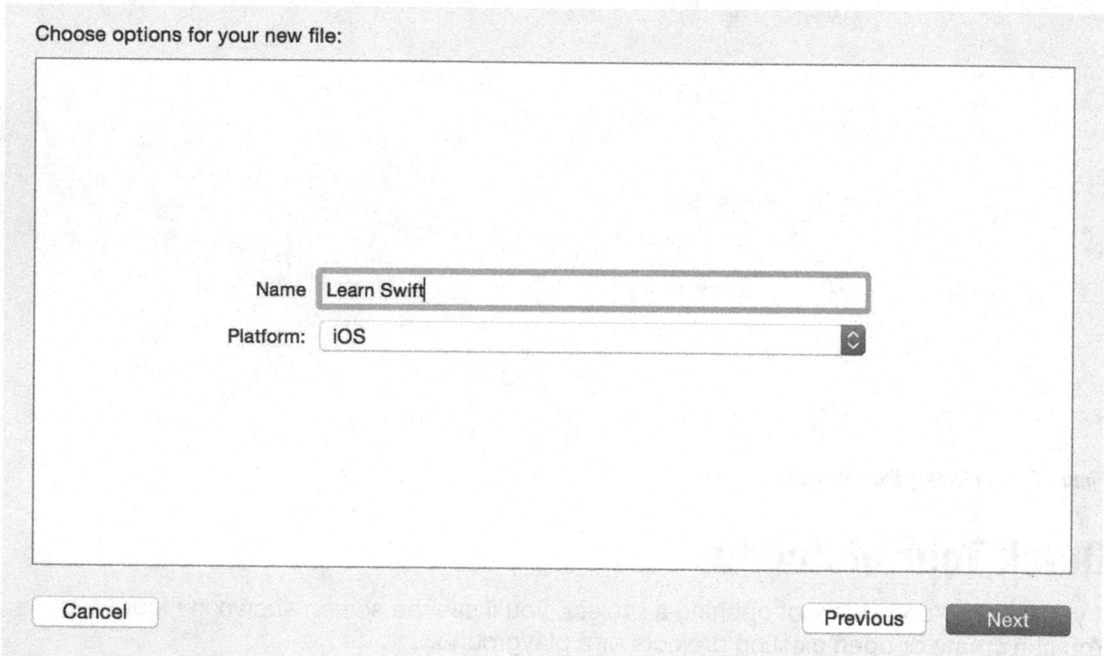

***Figure 1-4.** Naming a playground*

And now you're ready to play with Swift. As you can see in Figure 1-5, line numbers are not on by default. To turn them on—and set all of your text editing preferences—select **Xcode ➤ Preferences** again and then select the Text Editing tab. The first option you'll see lets you enable line numbers, so you'll be able to easily find a line as we discuss it.

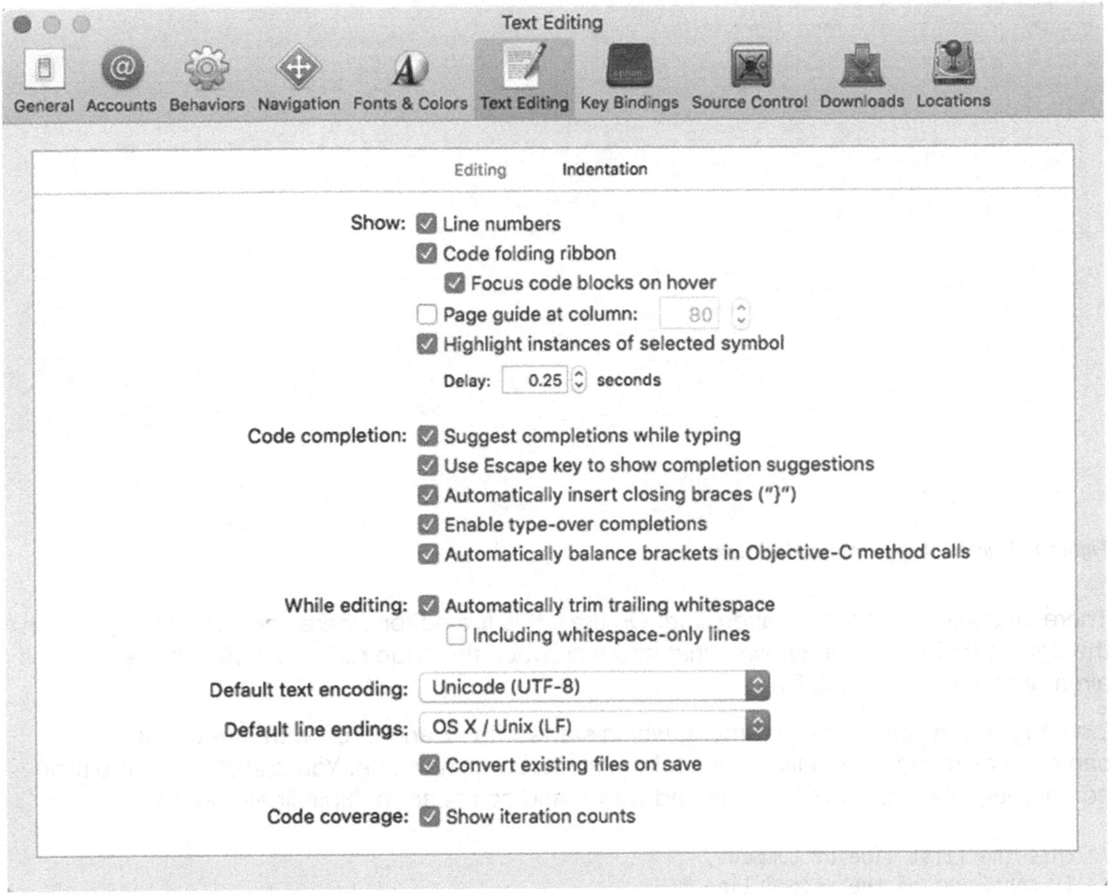

Figure 1-5. Setting text editing Preferences

Once you have created the playground and updated the preferences, you will be greeted by the playground window as shown in Figure 1-6.

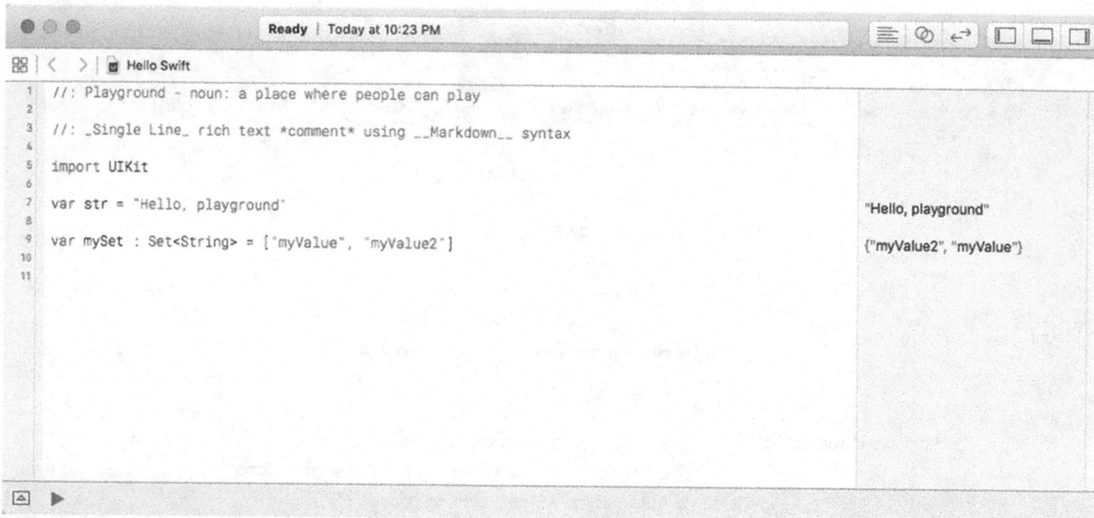

Figure 1-6. Interactive playground window

There are two parts to the playground. On the left is the editor where you write code, and on the right is a sidebar that shows what happens when the code runs. As you can see, there is already some code in the file.

Line 1 shows a single-line comment, which starts with // and ends with a new line. You can have as many as you like, but each must start on a new line. You can also use multiline comments, which start with /* and end with */ and can span multiple lines, like this:

```
/* this the first line of comment,
   it continues on the second line */
```

You can also have rich text comments using the markdown syntax; to use the rich text you simply start the comment by adding the : (colon)

```
//: _Single Line_ rich text *comment* using __Markdown__ syntax
```

The rendering is not turned on by default; you can enable that by selecting Editor ➤ Show Rendered Markup

Line 3 tells the compiler to import the iOS Cocoa Touch API so we can use it if we want to.

> **Note** Cocoa is the framework that defines the API for developing OS X applications. Cocoa Touch is the equivalent for iOS. Sometimes Cocoa is used to mean both OS X and iOS; and, in that case, the desktop version is referred to as AppKit.

Notice that there's no semicolon (;) at the end of the `import` statement. In Swift, semicolons are optional; they are required only if you put more than one statement on a single line, such as `var a = 4; var b = 8.`

Line 5 is a variable declaration, which shows the keyword var and the name of the variable and assigns the initial value to the variable. As you'd expect, the keyword var tells the compiler that I'm declaring a variable. Then I give it a name; the default name is *str* but it could be any valid string (discussed in a later chapter). You will notice that we did not define the type of the variable, because we are assigning an initial value of type that happens to be of type string, and the compiler will define str as of String type.

Quick Tour of Swift

Whenever you learn a new language, there's a long-standing tradition that your first program is one that displays "Hello, World." Let's stick with that tradition. In Swift, this takes just one line:

```
print("Hello, Swift!")
```

This is a complete Swift program, so you don't need to import a separate library to use the function. And you don't need a special entry point, such as the main function in Objective-C.

Basic Types

To create values, you use either let or var. The first keyword, let, creates a constant value, which can be assigned only once; var creates a variable whose value can change during the execution.

```
var myVariable = 11
myVariable = 33
let someOtherVariable = 22
```

Notice that we didn't give explicit types to these variables. They are implicitly inferred from the type of value they were assigned—integers in this case.

If the type information can't be derived from the initial value, then it must be specified. You do this by adding the type specifier after the variable, separated by a colon (:)

```
var implicitDoubleValue = 1.0
var explicitDoubleValue : Double = 22
var a, b, c : Float
```

Values are never implicitly converted from one type to another type. Every type that needs to convert to anther type must provide a conversion function. Look at the following code:

```
var myString = "The answer is "
let answer = 42
let myAnswer = myString + answer
```

Swift would give an error here. You have to use one of the String functions that converts an integer to a string:

```
let myAnswer = myString + String(answer) + "."
```

What this does is create a new string from answer, which is then appended to myString and provides the final answer:

```
print(myAnswer)
```

Another way to insert values into strings is to use the \() expression conversion function. To do this, you can write the expression:

```
let myAnswer = "The Answer is \(answer)."
```

The basic types are `String`, `Character`, `Int`, `UInt`, `Float`, and `Double`.

Collection Types

You can define arrays, sets, and dictionaries using bracket syntax.

```
var myArray : [String]()
var myDictionary : [String : String]()
var mySet : Set<String> = ["object", "object2"]
```

The types within the brackets are the type of values the collection can hold. Here we define the array to hold only string type values, and, for the dictionary, both the key and the value are of type `string`. But these don't have to be of type `string`; they can be `Int` or other collection types.

```
var myFavoriteFruits =["Oranges", "Bananas", "Grapes", "Mangos"]
myFavoriteFruits[2] = "Guavas"
var favorites = ["myFavorites" : myFavoriteFruits]
favorites["MishalsFavorite"] = ["Oranges", "Watermelon", "Grapes"]
favorites["AdamsFavorite"] = ["Apples", "Pears"]
```

Control Flow

You can choose `if`, `guard`, or `switch` for conditionals; and `for-in`, `for`, `while`, and `repeat-while` for loops. The parentheses around the conditional and loop variables are optional:

```
if a == b or if (a == b)
switch foo or switch (foo)
while a < b or while (a < b)
```

But the braces around the body are required:

```
if a == b
{
   print("they are equal")
}
```

Functions

The syntax for a function:

```
func functionName(arguments) -> returnType
{
}
```

or

```
func functionName(arguments)
{
}
```

In the second example, the function doesn't return a value. If you wanted to be pedantic, you could have a return type of Void; then the prototype would be func functionName(arguments) -> Void

> **Note** You also use the keyword func when defining methods for classes, structures, and enumeration types.

Functions in Swift are full-fledged types. You can pass them as arguments and return them from functions. You can have a function that takes a function and returns a function. There's a special kind of function called a closure. Functions are a special case of closures that has a name. You write the code for closures between {}:

```
{ (arguments) -> Int in /* body */ }
```

> **Note** In Objective-C the concept equivalent to closures is blocks. When interfacing with Objective-C from Swift, blocks are imported as closures.

Objects

Use the keyword class to define class objects, similar to functions:

```
class MyClass {
}
```

Classes in Swift don't require parent classes.

```
class myClass : ParentClass, Protocol, AnotherProtocol
{
}
```

Use enum to create enumeration types

```
enum MyEum: Int
{
  case One
  case Two
  case Three, Four, Five
}
```

The big difference in Swift for enums is they can include methods that operate on the cases of the enum and must have a type enum; types can be of non-integer types

```
enum TheEnum: String {
case Banana = "Banana"
case Grape = "Grape"
}
```

Use the `struct` keyword to define structs:

```
struct MyStruct
{
}
```

Structs support most of what classes can do. But the big difference between classes and structs is that when passing structs around the code, they are always copies, while classes are passed by reference.

Generics

Generic types are used when you design a class that can operate on different types of objects, which allows maximum reusability of the code. You can have a linked list of integers or characters or strings. In a language like Objective-C, you'd end up using *id* or *NSObject* to hold different types of objects. In Swift, you define your object with a generic type in angle brackets <>. Then, anytime you have to define a variable with a method or somewhere in your class, you use the type that was given in angle brackets. Typically, developers use `T` for type, but when you instantiate the class you have to give a proper type, such as `Int` or `Double` or `String`.

```
class Node<T>
{
  var value : T
}

var myNode : Node<Int>
```

In this example T is replaced with `Int`, and now Node can hold only `values of type` *Int*.

Getting the Sample Code

Xcode is a large application and will take some time to download and install. While you're waiting, you can download the sample code for this book from the Apress site. Go to `http://www.apress.com/book/view/9781484216286`. In the middle of the page below the book description, you'll see a tab that says `Source Code/Downloads`, where you'll find the download link. Click that link to download the source code to your preferred folder.

Summary

You should have everything you need to start playing with Swift or for developing your app. Don't forget to download the development tools and set up your development environment.

You've gotten just a quick overview of the Swift language, but there's lot more to come. Next, we are going to jump right in and start to play with Swift itself. By the end of this book, you'll be ready to write your great application in Swift.

Chapter 2

The Swift Playground in Xcode

The Swift playground is a new environment where the developers can view and manipulate their code live, instead of having to compile and run and test their code. You type your code and the compiler evaluates the code and gives you feedback right away; you can see the side effects. Think of it as a mini project with one file and an SDK to compile against.

> **Note** Other languages such as Scheme or Lisp have what is called REPL (read-eval-print-loop), which serves the same purpose.

This chapter will walk you through creating a playground and interacting with it. You will also create your first basic programs in Swift. We will be using playgrounds throughout this book whenever we need to demonstrate some code. It is much easier than edit-compile-run-loop.

We will also discuss the parts of the playground and what functionality they provide—and how to become really good at using playgrounds.

Getting Started with a Playground

If you don't have Xcode running, launch it; you will be greeted with the *Welcome to Xcode* screen. One of the options is to create a playground. Select the *Get started with a playground* to create a new playground. If you do not have *Welcome to Xcode* window visible, you can create a new playground by selecting the menu option **File ➤ New ➤ Playground**... or **Option-Shift-Command-N** key combination to get the creation dialog (Figure 2-1). We will start by creating a new OS X playground.

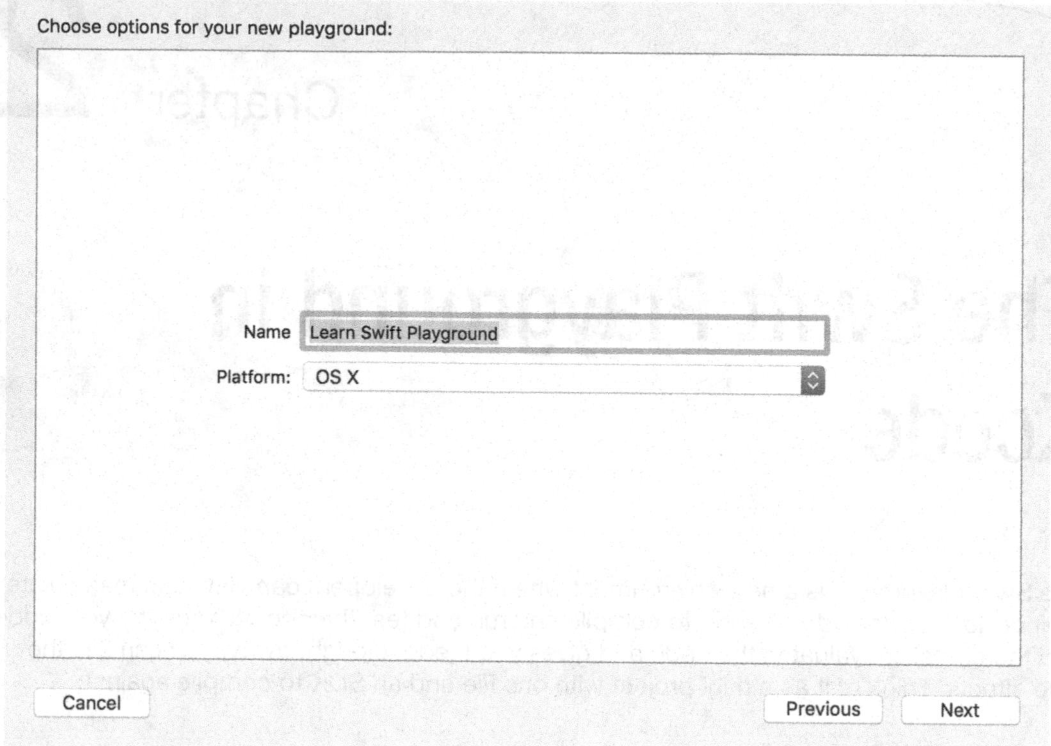

Figure 2-1. Playground Naming window

You will be greeted by the playground window shown in Figure 2-2. There are two parts to the playground: on the left is the editor, and on the right is the sidebar. When you create a new playground, it will already have some basic code. The code in the window is a complete Swift program.

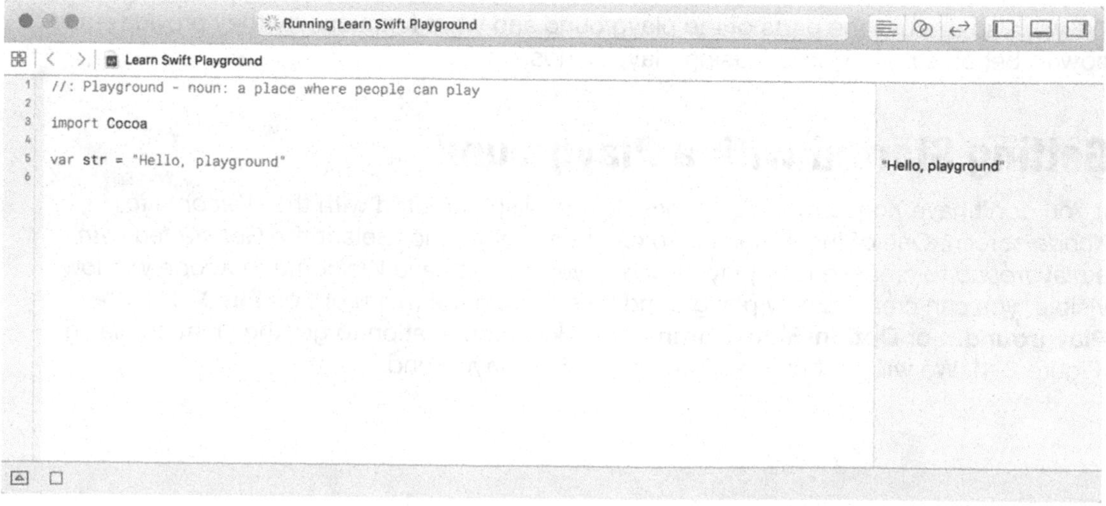

Figure 2-2. Playground Interaction window

The editor area is where you type your code into the playground. Then is the output from the complier with results.

Line 1 is a one of two types of comments. This one is called a single-line comment; it starts with // and ends with a new line. You can have as many as you like but they must start a new one on each line.

The other kind of comment is a multiline comment; it with a /* and ends with a */ and it can span multiple lines.

```
/* this the first line of comment,
   it continues on the second line */
```

Rich Text Comments

There is an extra colon (☺ right after the start of the comment (//). Xcode now supports comments in rich text using the Markdown format; if you add the colon then you can write the comment in Markdown format. However, they look the same. Let's update the comment to look like this: `//: Playground - **noun**: a place where people can *play*`

Next, select select menu option **Editor ➤ Show Rendered Markup;** you will see the comments with all the formatting.

Line 3 of the playground tells the compiler that we would like to import all desktop Cocoa APIs in case we decide to use them.

> **Note** Cocoa is the framework that defines the API for developing OS X applications. There is an equivalent for iOS called Cocoa touch. Sometimes Cocoa is collectively used for both OS X and iOS. You use UIKit for iOS and AppKit for OS X UI components.

You will notice that there is no semicolon (;) at the end of the `import` statement. This is because in Swift, the use of semicolons to terminate the statement is optional if you only have one statement on a line. If you put more than one statement on a line, then you must separate each statement with a semicolon, except for the last statement where the new line will terminate the statement. For example, you can do this `var a = 4; var b = 8`

Line 5 is a definition of a variable and then assignment of the value to that variable, the keyword `var` then the name of the variable followed by assignment of the initial value to the variable. Few things to notice here: the keyword var tells the compiler that I need to declare a variable, and then we give it a name. The default name is str but could be any valid string (which will discussed in a later chapter).

You will note that we did not give the type of variable such as `Int` or `Float`. That is because of type inference. What? It means that the type of variable is inferred by the kind of initial value that is assigned to it. Once the initial type is set for a variable, it cannot be changed. If you try to set an integer value to the variable `str`, the compiler will give you an error, as shown in line 6 of Figure 2-3.

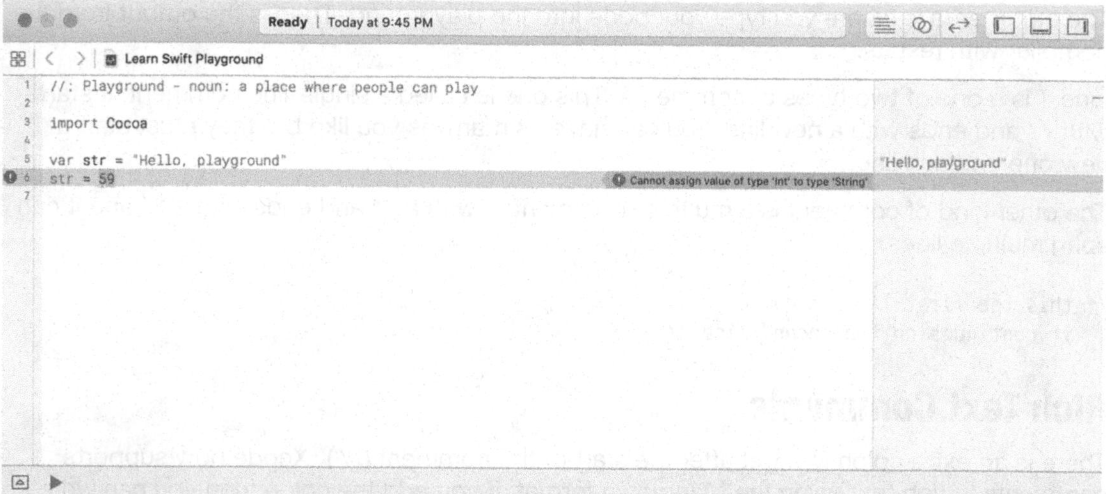
Ready | Today at 9:45 PM
Learn Swift Playground
//: Playground - noun: a place where people can play
import Cocoa
var str = "Hello, playground"
str = 59
Cannot assign value of type 'Int' to type 'String'
"Hello, playground"

Figure 2-3. Error when assigning wrong type

To assign an integer to a String type, we much convert it to a string first. We do this by creating a new string object using the initializer String(59), and now we are good to proceed.

Let's create another variable called `value` without assigning value (Figure 2-4). The compiler will report an error because Swift is a strongly typed language; it means that every variable must have a type associated with it. This will take care of lots of runtime errors that are associated with type conversation/coercion. When you are editing your code, if there is an error on the line, the editor will display a stop icon on the left of the line numbers. If you need to see the error message, you click on the icon so the error appears as shown in Figure 2-4.

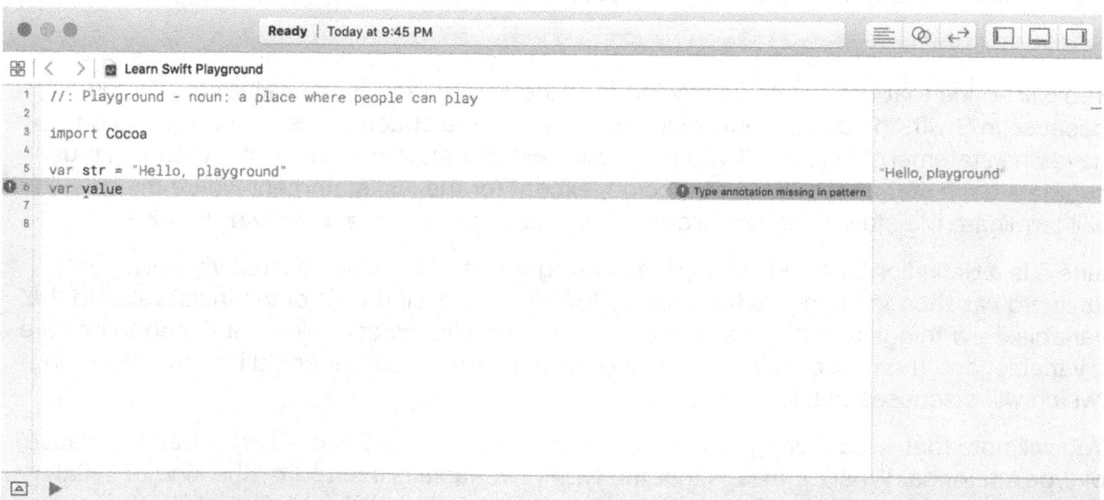
Ready | Today at 9:45 PM
Learn Swift Playground
//: Playground - noun: a place where people can play
import Cocoa
var str = "Hello, playground"
var value
Type annotation missing in pattern
"Hello, playground"

Figure 2-4. Missing Type Error

To give a type to a variable in Swift, you add the type after the variable name, separated by a colon. For example, when we write **var value : String,** this declares the variable value to be of type String. If you try to use this variable in an expression, the compiler will complain again. This time the issue is that the variable has not been initialized before using it. That is one of the Swift's safety requirements, as seen in Figure 2-5.

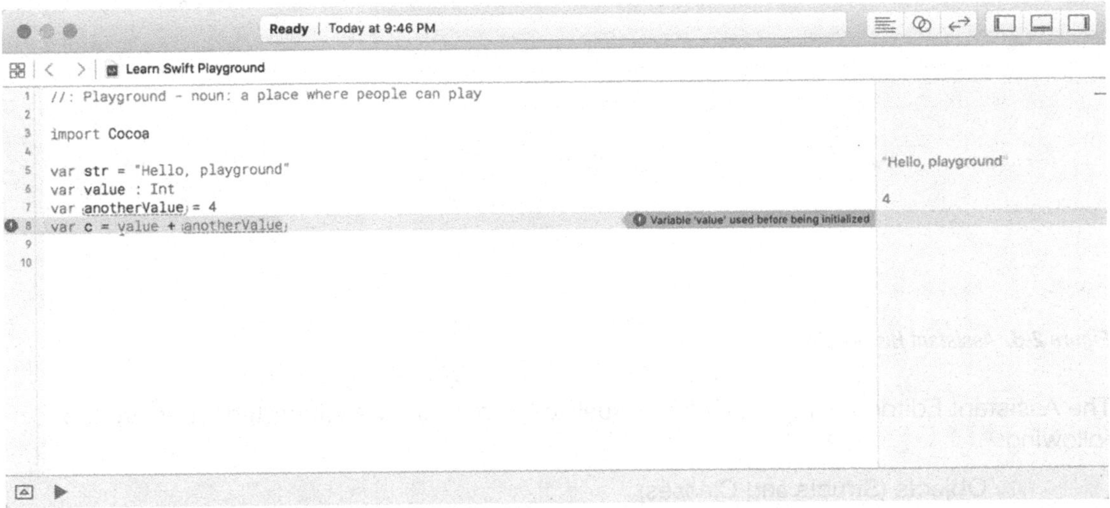

***Figure 2-5.** Uninitialized variable error*

On the right-hand side (sidebar) of the window, you will see the result of the statement on line 5; the result was that variable str was set to the string "Hello, playground."

If you hover over the value on line 5, you will see two icons on the right side of the line. The first, which looks like an eye, is the QuickLook. Clicking on it pops up a view of the object. The built-in types are supported, and you can also customize it for your own types. This is handy if the value is too long or complex to be displayed fully on the right side. The one that looks like a circle brings up the value history display in the Assistant Editor.

Type the following in the editor:

```
for i in 1...10 {
    i * i
}
```

Then select value history and in the Assistant Editor, you will get the visual representation of the loop, as shown in Figure 2-6.

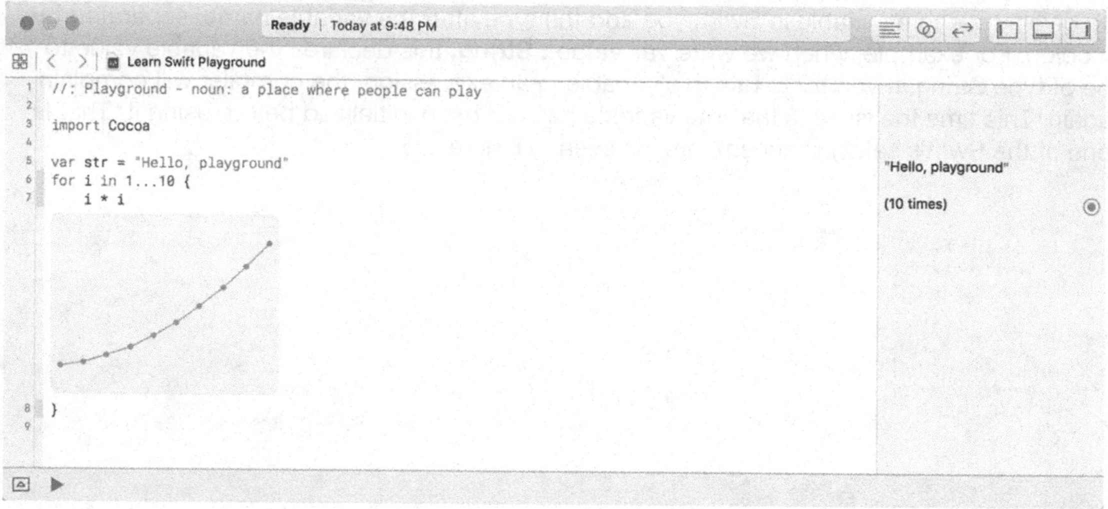

***Figure 2-6.** Assistant History View*

The Assistant Editor uses quick look to visualize the output. The supported types are the following:

- Objects (Structs and Classes)
- Strings
- Images
- Colors
- Views
- Array and Dictionaries
- Points, Rects, and Sizes
- Bézier Paths
- URLs (using WebView)

You can use the debugQuickLookObject function to display objects that are derived from NSObject, which are pretty much any existing Cocoa frameworks. Examples include UIImage, NSImage, UIColor, NSColor, UIView, and NSView. We will not list all the objects, but you get the idea.

Custom QuickLook Plug-Ins

Since you have not learned the language, this might be a bit difficult to understand, but this will show you how powerful playgrounds can be.

To develop custom plug-ins

you have to use XCPlayground module, which has three functions that will allow us to display custom values and views in the Assistant Editor.

> **Note** `XCPlayground` only works for `NSView`- and `UIView`-based subviews.

XCShowView

If you are developing a custom view and would like to show the results, you can call this method to display what the view looks like; it takes an identifier that is displayed at the top of the view so you know which view is being displayed.

```
XCShowView(identifier : String, view : NSView)
XCShowView(identifier : String, view : UIView)
```

XCCaptureValue

You are developing your program and you want to display some values; you can use this function to display the values.

XCCaptureValue<T>(identifier : String, value : T)

XCPSetExecutionShouldContinueIndefinitely

A common practice in mobile computing is client/server communication, but the network is inherently unreliable, so you to use asynchronous forms of communications where you make a call to the server. And when the server returns the response, you act on it. However, the call gets executed quickly and runs on the background thread. If you were to finish the tasks on the main thread, the program would exit, and we would not have a chance to process the response from the server. To keep the main program waiting for a response and not terminating the program, we use this function.

This function allows you to execute long running asynchronous tasks. One example is when you want to download some JSON data from the network.

```
XCPSetExecutionShouldContinueIndefinitely(continueIndefinitely: Bool = default)
```

Custom Modules for Playground

This is all good, but I have my own code, and I don't want to copy and paste into playground. I just want to use my classes in the playground. It is possible to do that, but these are the requirements:

- Code must be in a framework
- Classes you plan to use in playground must have public access
- Playground must be in the same workspace as the project with framework
- Framework must already be built
- For iOS it must be built for 64-bit runtime
- Must have a scheme that builds a target
- Build location preference must be set to Legacy
- Playground name must not be same as the build target

Importing Your Code

Once you have fulfilled these conditions, you can just `import ModuleName` to import your code into the playground.

We start by creating a framework first. Start Xcode and select "Create a new Xcode project" option shown in Figure 2-7.

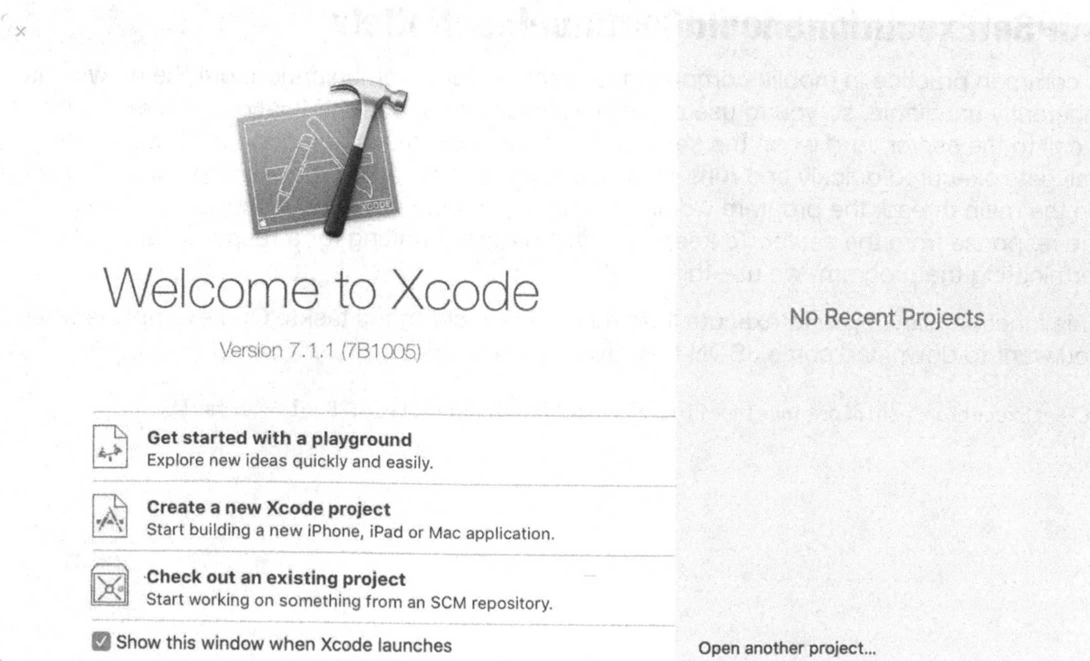

Figure 2-7. Xcode Welcome window

You will be asked to select the template for the project. Select under the iOS section Framework & Library, and then select Cocoa Touch Framework (Figure 2-8).

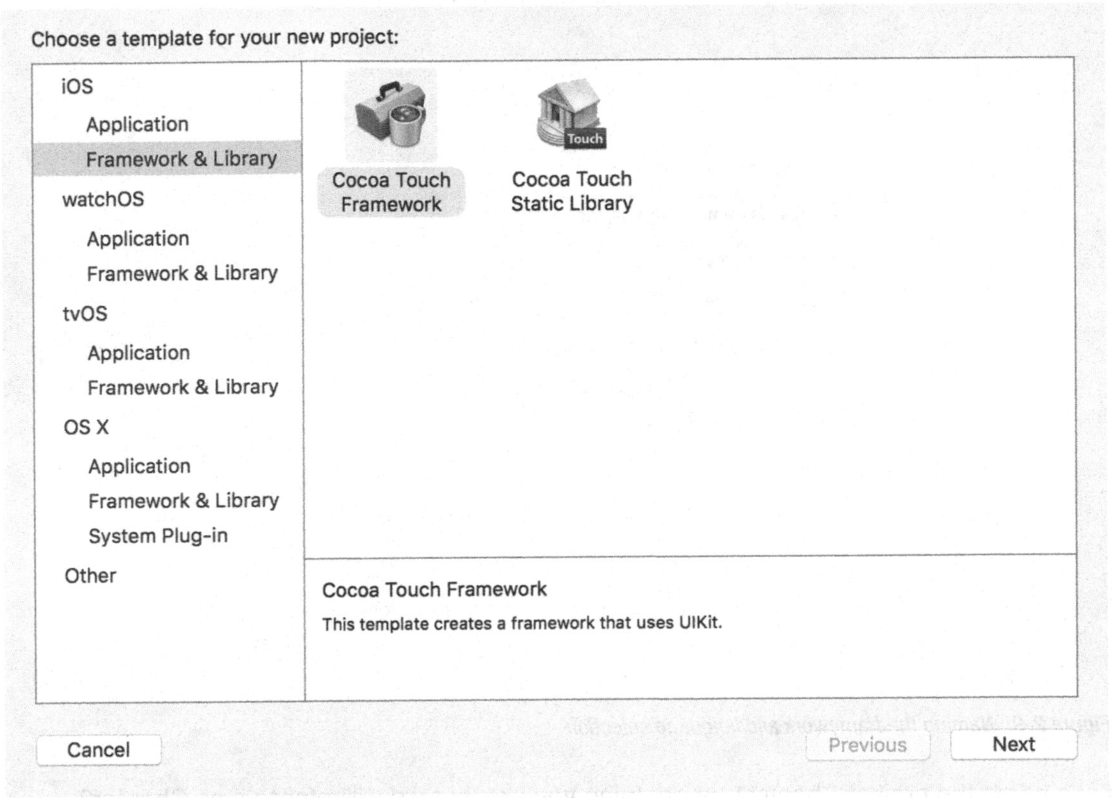

Figure 2-8. Project template selection window

Next step: you are asked to give the framework a name and other information. Make sure to select Swift under the Language option (Figure 2-9).

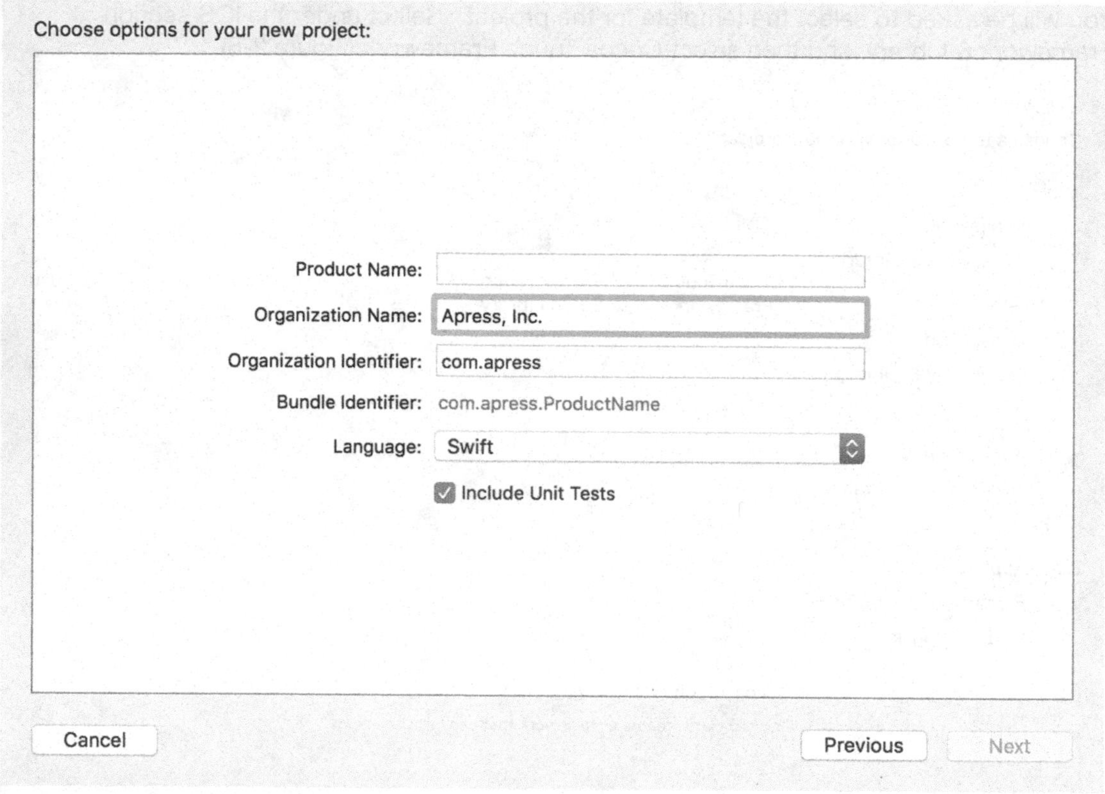

***Figure 2-9.** Naming the framework and language selection*

Let's name the project Chapter1, or anything you like, but we will refer to it as Chapter2.

Once you have saved the project you will be ready to code. We also need a workspace. A workspace is where you combine your frameworks and sources. To create a workspace from an existing open project, select from the **File ➤ Save as Workspace...** option and give it the same name as the project. Typically you name the workspace the same as the main project, so let's name it Chapter2 and save it in the same location as the project file. Now you will have two files: one called Chapter2.xcworkspace and Chapter2.xcodeproj. From now on, always open the workspace if you need to work on the project.

Next we need to create some types for your framework that we will use in the playground. Create a new file by selecting **File ➤ New ➤ File...** make sure to select iOS ➤ Source and then Swift File.

> **Note** You can also import your existing files into the framework.

We added the following code:

```
public class Chapter2
{
    var message : String
    public init(_ message : String)
    {
        self.message = message
    }

    public func printMessage()
    {
        println(message)
    }
}
```

Next we need to add an example project that has our framework as a dependency. **File ➤ New ➤ Target...**, choose **iOS ➤ Application ➤ Single View Application** (Figure 2-10).

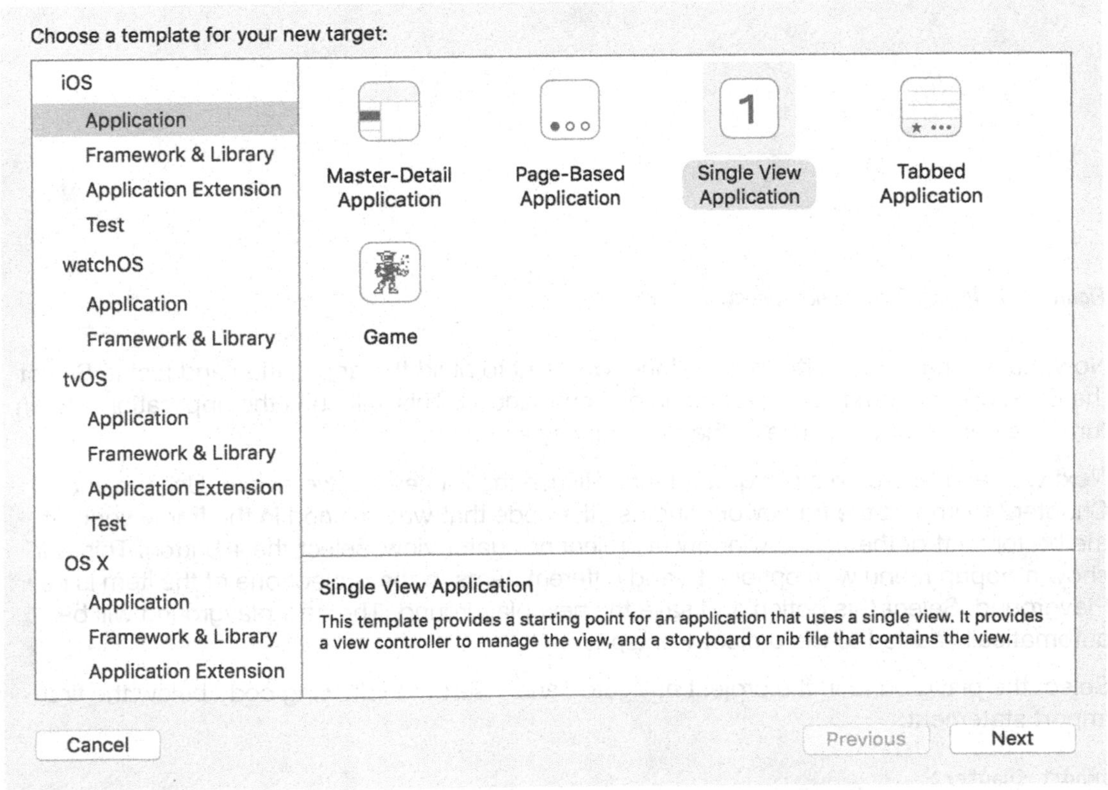

***Figure 2-10.** iOS Application Template window*

Give it the name Chapter2Example (Figure 2-11); now we need to have the app depend on our framework. Select the project and then select Chapter2Example target. One of the options is Build Phases, where we are going to add dependency.

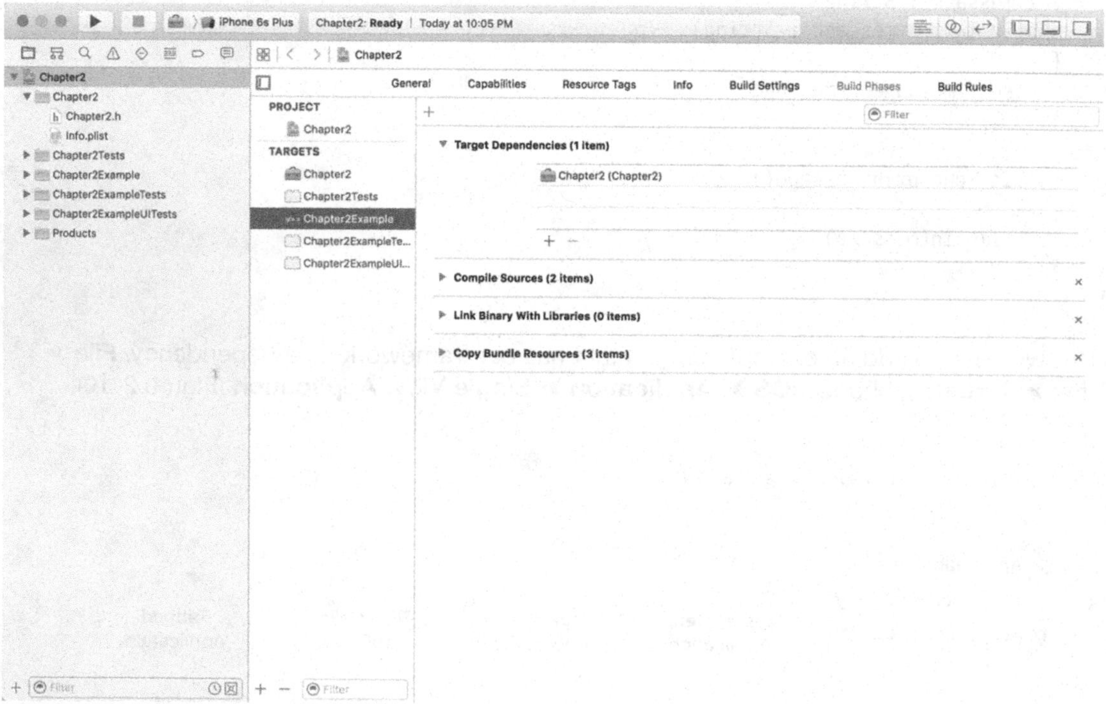

Figure 2-11. *Project Dependency window*

Now that we have the settings part done, we need to build the application and test it. Select the Build option from the project menu or Command-B. This will build the application and, in turn, the framework because of the dependency setup.

Next we need to create a playground that will use the framework we create. Use the import Chapter2 to import the framework and use the code that was defined in the framework. At the bottom left of the Xcode window in project navigator view, select the + button. This will show a popup menu with options to add different items to the project one of the item is new Playground. Select this option and save the new playground. The new playground will be automatically added to the project workspace.

Select the playground in the project navigator, and insert the following code below the first import statement:

```
import Chapter2
var hello = Chapter2("Hello, framework")
hello.printMessage()
```

If you open the Assitant Editor, you will see output from the framework Keep in mind that if you change any code in the framework you will need to build the application so that the framework gets rebuilt. If you do not do this step the new code will not be available in the playground.

Summary

You learned what Swift playgrounds are and how they can help you develop code visually. You learned how to create a framework and have the project depend on the framework. And you also learned how to import your framework into your playground. You can also share your playground just like you can share your projects.

Playgrounds are good for learning and doing quick prototyping of your code, but they have limitations:

- Not good for performance testing
- You can't interact with views

Can't run on devices

Chapter 3

Accessing Swift's Compiler and Interpreter: REPL

Let's now investigate how to access the Swift compiler from the command-line interface known as the **R**ead-**E**val-**P**rint-**L**oop, or REPL. This is where you can interact with the compiler by entering statements, which the compiler will interpret and evaluate immediately.

What Is REPL?

The REPL is an interactive shell similar to the UNIX shell and those of other languages such as Lisp, Ruby, and Python. When you start the shell, you are given a prompt to enter your code. The compiler interprets and evaluates the entered code and then prints either the result or an error.

If you don't have Terminal in the Dock, locate the Terminal app in the Utilities folder and drag it to the Dock, then launch it by selecting it from the Dock.

With Terminal running, you access REPL by simply typing **swift** at the command prompt. Assuming the Xcode command-line tools have been set up correctly, you'll then see the Swift welcome message, like this:

```
tardis:~ malik$ swift
Welcome to Apple Swift version 2.1 (700.1.101.6 700.1.76). Type :help for assistance.
  1>
```

If that doesn't work, try entering **xcrun swift.** If you still get an error, Swift is probably not set up correctly.

```
tardis:~ malik$ swift
swift: error: unable to find utility "swift", not a developer tool or in PATH
```

To fix the missing command-line tools problem you can use a utility called `xcode-select`; this utility is installed when you install and run the Xcode. To test whether the command-line tools were installed correctly, use the following command to find which version of the command-line tools is being used:

```
tardis:~ malik$ xcode-select --print-path
/Applications/Xcode.app/Contents/Developer
```

If you are running an older version of Xcode, or more than one version, you will want to select Xcode 7 or later for the command-line tools. You can do this from the command line using the xcode-select command:

```
tardis:~ malik$ sudo xcode-select -switch /Applications/Xcode.app
```

You can also do it by going to **Xcode ➤ Preferences** and selecting the Locations tab, as shown in Figure 3-1.

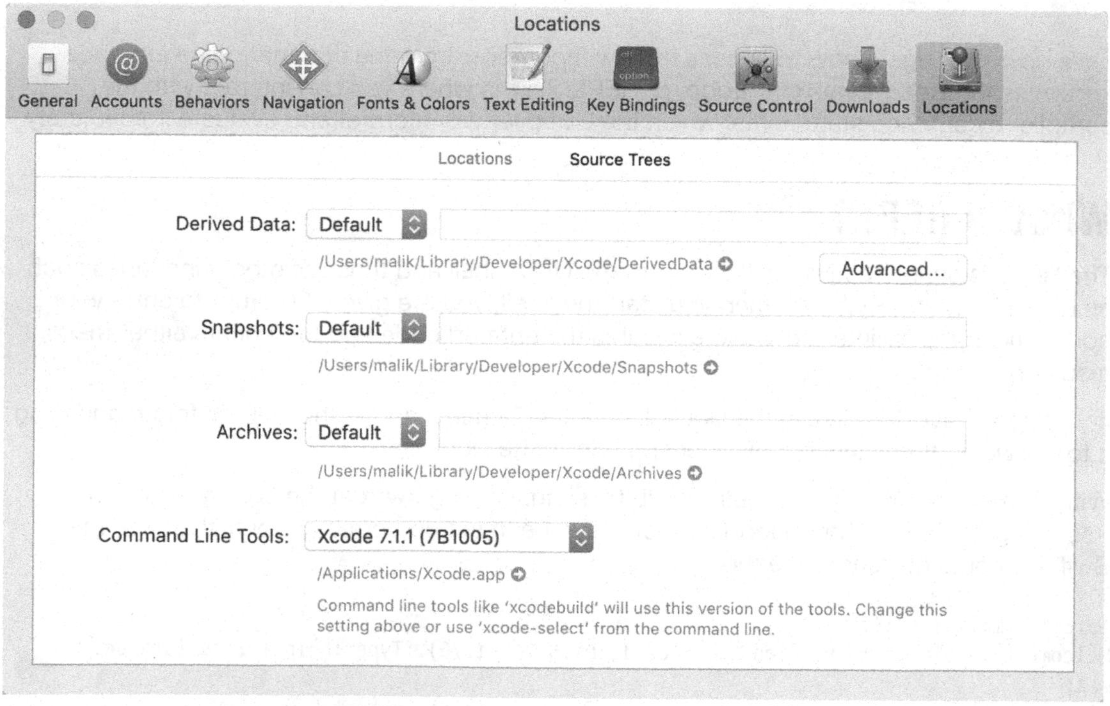

***Figure 3-1.** Selecting the Command-Line Tools version*

This will set the location of the command-line tools that are part of the Xcode.app package.

Once you've set the paths correctly and are at the Swift prompt in the REPL, you can enter the code you want the compiler to interpret. When you're finished playing with the REPL, just type **:quit** and you'll be back in your previous shell.

LLDB and the Swift REPL

You can also use the REPL in LLDB, which is the default debugger in Xcode. If you're running a program, you'll have to pause execution of the program to get to the debugger prompt. Once the program has stopped, either at a breakpoint in your program or because you selected the pause button in the debug window, just type **repl** to get the REPL.

```
(lldb) repl
>
```

To get back to LLDB just type a colon : and press Enter and you'll be back in the debugger.

```
  1> var a = "Hello"
a: String = "Hello"
  2> var b = "REPL"
b: String = "REPL"
  3> println(a +
  4. ", " + b)
Hello, REPL
  5>
```

You can also compile your program using the command-line compiler `swiftc`, or run your script using the Swift REPL. To run the script use the swift command with the source file.

```
swift hello.swift
```

There are quite a few options for the interpreter. Type **swift -help** to display the options and get help specific to the Swift application. The basic command structure is **swift [options] <inputs>** where [options] are any of the listed options that were displayed using the -help option. For example, if you wanted to link to a custom framework, you will need to use the **-framework <name>** option.

When looking at these options, note that the values between the square brackets [] are optional and those between the angle brackets <> are required. You replace them, including the brackets, with your specific values. In the following example, we run script in the `mylocation.swift` source file and link with the CoreLocation.framework. If you have custom framework you will need to specify the path to where the framework is located. For system provided frameworks you don't need to give the path

```
tardis:~ malik$ swift -framework CoreLocation.framework mylocation.swift
```

This example will not create an executable, it just interprets the statement. To compile the file and make it executable, you will need to use the Swift compiler, `swiftc`. Let's give it a try.

Create a file using your favorite editor and name it Hello.swift. Now add the following code:

```
print("Hello, Compiler")
```

This is a simple program that prints a message. After you've added the code and saved the file, compile the file using the following command:

```
tardis:Chapter3 malik$ swiftc Hello.swift -o Hello
```

This command compiles `Hello.swift` and outputs an executable—a stand-alone program called `Hello`. Now you can take this program and run it without the Swift interprter. That's the difference between an interpreter and a compiler. To the run the executable, you just type its name. If you get an error because your current path is not part of your PATH variable, just tell the interpreter that the file is located in the current directory by prepending ./ to the name of the executable:

```
tardis:Chapter3 malik$ ./Hello
Hello, Compiler
```

Now add the following line of code, keeping in mind that once you've edited the file, you have to recompile it to re-create the executable with new code. If you don't, either you will not have an executable or have an executable that was compiled with previous iteration of the code.

```
print("Hello, Again)
tardis:Chapter3 malik$ swiftc Hello.swift -o Hello
Hello.swift:2:7: error: unterminated string literal
print("Hello, Again)
     ^

Hello.swift:2:21: error: expected ',' separator
print("Hello, Again)
                ^
                ,
Hello.swift:3:1: error: expected expression in list of expressions

^
Hello.swift:2:21: error: expected ',' separator
print("Hello, Again)
                ^
```

, Oh no, that doesn't look good. Can you guess what happened? Yes, that's correct. There's an error in the code; the compiler is kind enough to tell us where we have made the mistake.

First, it indicates that the error is in the Hello.swift file. In this case, that's the only file, but if you're compiling more than one file, this message is helpful. The next two numbers, :5:1:, are the row and column in the file where the error was triggered, followed by the actual error message from the compiler, indicating that the string is missing the closing quote of the string. Finally, the next two lines show the actual line of the code and a ^ where the error was triggered.

```
println("Hello, Compiler")

println("Hello, Again")
swiftc Hello.swift -o Hello
tardis:Chapter3 malik$ ./Hello
Hello, Compiler
Hello, Again
```

Success! After I recompiled the file, everything worked as expected.

Summary

You learned how to set up the command-line tools. This will give you access to both the Swift compiler and interpreter. You found out what REPL is and how Swift can be accessed from the Terminal app and the LLDB debugger using the REPL. Finally, you learned how to compile a swift file using the compiler to generate an executable program.

Chapter 4

Constants, Variables, and Data Types

In OOP languages, an immutable object is an object whose state can't be modified. Swift calls these constants. Once a constant object has been created and an initial value has been assigned, the object cannot be changed. In contrast, an object whose value can be changed is a mutable object, or the object can be mutated. Swift calls these objects variables.

In Swift, when defining variables they must be initialized with a valid value before they can be used. Use the `var` keyword to define a mutable object and the `let` keyword to define an immutable object. Note that all types can be defined either as mutable or immutable (constant or variable) based on whether they're defined with `let` or `var keyword`. The language doesn't require separate mutable and immutable types:

```
let numberOfWheelsForBicycle = 2
var numberOfPassengers = 1
```

You can also declare multiple values on a single line:

```
var a = 2.0, b = 5.0, c = 3.0
```

> **Note** If **object** values aren't going to change, always declare them as constants using the **let** keyword. The compiler will also let you know.

Type Annotation

So far we have not provided the types for the variables, since Swift will infer the type from the initial value assigned to the variable. However, you can specify the type of the variable explicitly.

> **Note** Swift is a strong typed language, which means that each variable must have a type associated with it.

```
var songName : String
```

This statement declares a mutable variable named `songName` of type `String`. We are telling the compiler that `songName` will store values only of type `String`. You typically need to do this if Swift can't infer the type of variable.

Once the variable type has been assigned, it cannot be changed. You cannot declare a variable of type `String` and then assign a value of type number, even though you have not assigned an initial value. Once the variable is declared in a scope, you cannot redeclare it in the same scope even with the same type.

Identifiers

The name given to a constant or a variable is called an identifier. Swift is designed to use almost any character, including Unicode characters, for names. However, identifiers cannot start with numbers or contain:

- Mathematical symbols (+, -, and so on)
- Arrows
- Private-use Unicode points
- Invalid Unicode points
- Line- or box- drawing characters

```
let Ω = "Omega"
let π = 3.1415
var 🐘 = "Elephant"
var radius = 4.0
var circumference = 2 * π * radius
```

Console Output

Now that you have these values, how do you print them? Swift provides a global function called `print`. The print function takes an array of objects that can be converted to a string.

```
print("Hello, This is a long string")
```

To embed a value in a string, you can wrap it with a backslash and parentheses:

```
print("The area of circle = \(areaOfCircle)")
print("Area of Circle = ")
print(areaOfCircle)
```

The full definition of the print function is:

```
print(items: Any..., separator: String = default, terminator: String = default)

var hello = "Hello"
var playground = "playground"
print(hello, playground)
```

The default separator is space " " and the default terminator is new line character. You can specify either of those, for instance: if you do not want to print a new line at the end, you can change terminator to ""; or if you wanted to print each object on a new line you can change the separator to "\n".

```
print(hello, playground, separator: "\n", terminator: "")
```

> **Note** All string manipulations like this can be used anywhere a string literal is used.

Integers

Almost everyone is familiar with whole numbers also known as integers. You can define two types of whole numbers: signed or unsigned.

Z = {..., -3, -2, -1, 0, 1, 2, 3, ...}

N0 = {0, 1, 2, 3, ...}

Swift provides integers of different sizes based on the number of bits. The ranges of values that can be assigned are based on the size. You can get the min and max value for each of these using the `.min` and `.max` functions

```
Int8, Int16, Int32, Int64, UInt8, UInt16, UInt32, UInt64,
println(UInt8.min)
println(UInt8.max)
println(Int8.min)
println(Int8.max)
```

Two other integer types are also available: `Int` and `UInt`. The range of values for these depends on the hardware architecture:

- On 32-bit machines, `Int` is the same as `Int32`.
- On 64-bit machines, `Int` is the same size as `Int64`.

Similarly `UInt` is `UInt32` on 32-bit machines and `UInt64` on 64-bit machines.

Floating-Point Numbers

Floating points numbers have fractional parts, such as π, 0.345, and 342.9495. These numbers can represent a much larger set of values. Swift provides two floating-point types; the different is in precision.

- `Float` is defined using 32 bits of data.
- `Double` is defined using 64 bits of data.

Numeric Literals

You can create numeric literals in various bases using a prefix:

- Decimal numbers have no prefix.
- Binary numbers use the 0b prefix.
- Octal numbers use the 0o prefix.
- Hexadecimal numbers use the 0x prefix.

Floating-point literals can be expressed in decimal or hexadecimal. For decimal, the literal comprises a set of decimal digits (with a decimal point). The exponent is a power of 10, separated by the letter "e." 12e2 is the same as 12 * 10^2 or 1200.0. For hexadecimal, the value starts with the 0x and the exponent is a power of 2, separated by p for power; 0xap3 is same as 0xa * 2^3 or 40. The exponent can be negative or positive, depending on whether you're multiplying or dividing.

```
var exp0 = 12e2
var exp1 = 0xap2
var exp2 = 12e-2
var exp3 = 0xap-2
```

When writing long numbers, you can separate them using the underscore (_) to make them easier to read. This is purely for human readability. The compiler will strip out the underscore and make a valid number:

```
let million = 1_000_000
let billion = 1_000_000_000
let floating = 1_0.933_39484
```

Conversion

Because one of the central goals of the Swift language is safety, there are only a very few situations where a number's type can be converted automatically. For the most part, you must do an explicit conversion when mixing different types of numbers. The process of converting from one type to another is called casting.

When casting from a larger value to a smaller one, the smaller value will not be able to hold the larger value if a larger number's value is larger than the maximum value the smaller can hold. This is called an overflow, which in Swift is not safe, so automatic casting is not allowed most of the time.

If you need to mix numbers of different types in an expression, you'll have to convert one of them to the other's type before you can combine them. You can do that by using the constructor for type:

```
var  million : Int = 1_000_000_000
var floating : Float = 453.20
var ac = million + floating // Error
var ab = million + Int(floating)
```

The expression `Int(floating)` will convert the floating-point number to an integer. This is done by creating an integer from a floating type.

> **Note** By default, the compiler will create a `Double` for a `floating` type. If you actually want a `Float`, you will have to specify the `Float` type: `var myFloat : Float`

Booleans

Swift has a Boolean type called `Bool`, which provides either `true` or `false` values. Some languages, notably C based, use 0 (zero) as false and any other value for true. In Swift that is not the case; either it can be true or false and nothing else.

```
var theBool = true

if theBool == true {
    print("true")
} else {
    print("false")
}
```

Characters

Characters in Swift represent a single Unicode character. You can define a character using:

```
let automobile : Character = "🚘"
```

If you don't specify the type, the type inference will create a string type, so for characters you have to either specify the type or express the characters in hexadecimal using the following:

- Single-byte Unicode character \xnn
- Double-byte Unicode character \unnnn
- Four-byte Unicode character \Unnnnnnnn

Strings

Strings are a sequence of character types:

```
let message = "This is a string"
```

There are special characters that must be specified by escaping with a backslash:

- Null character \0
- Backslash \\
- Horizontal Tab \t
- Line feed \n
- Carriage return \r
- Double Quote \"
- Single Quote \'

To create an empty string, you can define:

```
var string1 = ""
var string2 = String()
```

The `String` class is compatible with the Objective-C `NSString` class. You can substitute `String` for `NSString` in the API calls and use methods such as `isEmpty`, `hasPrefix`, and `hasSuffix` on string types.

```
if string1.isEmpty {
    print("This is an empty string")
}
string1 = "Learn Swift 2 on the Mac"
if string1.hasPrefix("Learn") {
    print("The string starts with \"Learn\"")
}

if false == string1.hasSuffix("Learn") {
    print("The string does not end in \"Learn\"")
}
```

The mutability of the strings depends on how they are created. If strings are created using the `let` keyword they are constants; if they're created using `var`, strings are mutable.

> **Note** In Objective-C it's different. You use either of the two classes `NSString` and `NSMutableString`, depending on whether you want a constant or mutable string.

You can concatenate strings and characters with the + operator. You can also use the += to append to an existing string:

```
string1 = string1 + " by Waqar Malik"
string1 += " by Waqar Malik"
string1.appendContentsOf(" by Waqar Malik")
```

To count characters, use the global function count on characters:

```
let animals = "🐖🐘🐍🐢🐛🐝🐜🐞🐌🐠🐟🐬🐳🐋🐂🐏🐃🐅🐇🐎"
print("Number of characters \(animals.characters.count)")
```

To iterate over the characters in the string, you can use the for-in loop (discussed later):

```
for animal in animals {
    print(animal)
}
```

Two strings are considered equal if they have exactly the same characters in the same order:

```
let bookTitle1 = "Learn Swift 2 on the Mac"
var bookTitle2 = "Learn Swift 2 on the Mac"
if bookTitle1 == bookTitle2 {
    print("They are the same")
}

bookTitle2 = "Learn swift 2 on the Mac"
if bookTitle1 == bookTitle2 {
    print("They are the same")
}
```

In the second example, the strings are not the same, because Swift starts with a lowercase character. For computers, S and s are not the same characters.

When comparing strings, if you don't care about the case sensitivity of a string, convert both strings to either uppercase or lowercase and then compare:

```
if bookTitle1.uppercaseString == bookTitle2.uppercaseString {
    print("They are the same")
}
```

Collection Types

Swift provides various collection types, arrays, sets, and dictionaries.

Arrays

Arrays store multiple values of the same type in an ordered list. The values can be repeated in the list. Arrays in Swift are different from Objective-C:

- Mutability is defined using the `let` or `var` declaration.
- All values in the array must be of the same type.

> **Note** NSArray holds objects of type NSObject, which, when imported into Swift, are translated as AnyObject.

There are two ways you can define an array type variable:

- `var array : Array<String>`
- `var array : [String]`

The second one is shorthand for creating, in this case, an array of type `String`. If you try to insert an object of a type other than `String`, the compiler will give an error.

```
var someFruits : Array<String> = ["Banana", "Apple", "Pear", "Watermelon", "Mango", "Kiwi"]
var someFruits : [String] = ["Banana", "Apple", "Pear", "Watermelon", "Mango", "Kiwi"]
```

You don't have to specify the type if you initialize the array with at least one value so the type can be inferred. The previous declaration can be done by omitting: `[String]` or: `Array<String>`:

```
var someFruits = ["Banana", "Apple", "Pear", "Watermelon", "Mango", "Kiwi"]
```

We created an array with the names of some fruits. We can append more items to the array using the append method:

```
someFruits.append("Guava")
someFruits += ["Grapes"]
```

The first line appends one element, and the second line appends an array of one element of the same type.

Use the `isEmpty` property to check if the array is empty:

```
if someFruits.isEmpty {
    print("Array is empty")
} else {
    print("Array is not empty")
}
```

You can retrieve the elements using the subscript syntax:

```
let thirdItem = someFruits[2]
```

As you can see, the arrays use a zero-based index. Since this array is mutable, let's replace some elements. I really wanted grapes instead of bananas:

```
someFruits[0] = "Grapes"
```

You can also replace values in the original array by giving a range. Here are the beginning values: `["Banana", "Apple", "Pear", "Watermelon", "Mango", "Kiwi"]`

To replace items 2 through 4, use:

```
someFruits[2...4] = ["Peaches", "Oranges"]
```

The array now holds these values: `[Banana, Apple, Peaches, Oranges, Kiwi]`

What this did was replace the three items at locations 2, 3, and 4 with two new items, reducing the size of the array by one.

You can increase the size of the array by providing more items on the right side of the expression. The following will increase the size of the original array by replacing the items given by the specified range:

```
someFruits[2...3] = ["Guava", "Plum", "Fig"]
```

After the insertion, the array looks like this:

```
[Banana, Apple, Guava, Plum, Fig, Kiwi]
```

To insert an item at given location in an array use the method `insert`:

```
someFruits.insert("Nectarines", atIndex: 3)
```

To remove an item from the list, use the method `remove`:

```
someFruits.removeAtIndex(1)
someFruits.removeLast()
```

You can iterate over the entire array using a for-in loop:

```
for fruit in someFruits {
    print(fruit)
}
```

If you'd like to get the index of an item along with the item itself, use the `enumerate` global function on the array. The `enumerate` function returns a tuple (disused later) with an index and value for each item:

```
for (index, fruit) in someFruits.enumerate() {
    print("Fruit at index \(index + 1) is \(fruit)")
}
```

You can also create arrays of a given size and a given initial value. To initialize an array of floats of size 10, with initial values of 1.0, you can use a convenience initializer:

```
var myFloats = [Float](count: 10, repeatedValue: 1.0)
// [1.0, 1.0, 1.0, 1.0, 1.0, 1.0, 1.0, 1.0, 1.0, 1.0]
```

Sets

A set type is similar to an array type with two differences:

- The order of the elements is not defined.
- Repeating on the elements is not allowed.

In an array you can insert the elements in order and that order will be preserved. If you inserted a value at location 1, when you later retrieved the value from location 1, you will get the same value, but a set inserting a given location is not allowed.

Arrays allow you to add the same object/value at different locations.

```
var array = [1]
array.append(1)
print(array.count) // this will print count of elements = 2
var set : Set<Int> = [1]
set.insert(1)
print(set.count) // this will print count of elements = 1
```

Dictionaries

Dictionaries store values of the same type, but they associate each value with a unique key. The keys can't be repeated but the values can be. Think of each key as the index into an array. Unlike with arrays, however, the items don't have an order. For dictionaries you must specify the key type and value type the dictionary will store:

```
var states : Dictionary<String, String> = ["CA" : "California"]
var states : [String : String] = ["CA" : "California"]
```

Both of these define a dictionary states that has a key type of String and value type of String. You don't need to specify the type of the key and value if you initialize the array with values:

```
var states = ["CA" : "California"]
var states = ["CA" : "California", "NV" : "Nevada", "OR": "Oregon", "AZ" : "Arizona"]
```

You can access values of the dictionary by using the key subscript:

```
states["NV"] = "Nevada"
```

or

```
let value = states["NV"]
```

To change the existing value, you set the value using the same key

```
states["NV"] = "State of Nevada"
states.updateValue("State of Nevada", forKey: "NV")
```

Both of these lines update the value of the key "NV," but there's one difference—the `updateValue` function returns the old value. So you could use:

```
let oldValue = states.updateValue("State of Nevada", forKey: "NV")
```

If the value for the key doesn't exist, these calls will add it to the dictionary. The `updateValue` function will return `nil` if the key does not exist in the dictionary.

To remove values from the dictionary, you can use the subscript method and assign the `nil` value to a given key or use the `removeValueForKey` function.

```
states["TX"] = nil
```

Or

```
states.removeValueForKey("TX")
```

The `removeValueForKey` function will return the value it replaced or `nil` if the key doesn't exist.

As with arrays, you can iterate over the entire dictionary using the for-in loop:

```
for (key, value) in states {
    print("State name = \(value), abbreviation = \(key)")
}
```

You can also iterate over just the keys or the values as arrays using the properties keys and `values`:

```
for abbreviation in states.keys {
    print("Abbreviation = \(abbreviation)")
}

for name in states.values {
    print("Name = \(name)")
}
```

If you'd like to use your own object as a key, the object must be hashable; that is, it must conform to the hashable protocol. This means it must implement a property called `hashValue` that returns an integer value, a value that identifies the object. A `hashValue` doesn't need to be unique, but the value does need to be chosen so that different objects do not have the same `hashValue`. The object must also implement the equality (==) operator.

Swift's built-in data types, such as `String`, `Int`, `Double`, and `Bool` are hashable, which means you can use them for keys.

Tuples

Tuples are groups of ordered values, possibly of different types. You can have named or unnamed tuples, which differ in how you access the elements:

```
let myUnnamedTuple = ("Name", 4.24, 10)
```

This creates a tuple that has three values, and you can see that each is a different type. To access an individual item in the tuple, you can either reference it by index or by decomposing the tuple to names:

```
println(myUnnamedTuple.0)
println(myUnnamedTuple.1)
println(myUnnamedTuple.2)

let (title, value, other) = myUnnamedTuple
print(title)
print(value)
print(other)
```

You assign a name to each item in the tuple and then access the items using those names. This involves some extra code that's not required if you use named tuple values. To do so, you assign a name to each item in the tuple and then access items using those names:

```
let myNamedTuple = (title: "Name", value: 4.25, other: 10)
print(myNamedTuple.title)
print(myNamedTuple.value)
print(myNamedTuple.other)
```

All of this code is using type inference, but if you want to be explicit about what types the values use you can specify the types:

```
let namedAndTypedTuple : (title : String, value : Float, other : UInt) = ("Name", 4.25, 10)
```

Tuples are useful when you're returning multiple values from functions; you've already seen that with the `enumerate` function for the dictionary type.

Optionals

The concept of optionals is new. There's no equivalent in C or Objective-C—the closest thing is `nil` in Objective-C. Any type in Swift can be declared optional by adding the ? to the type. But, what does that mean?

In Swift, every variable must have a valid value in order to be used, because of the safety requirements of the language. But there are times when you may not have a valid value for a variable. In that case, you declare the variable as an optional, meaning that if the variable doesn't have a value, it will be `nil`; otherwise it will have a valid value. In other words, `Int?` boxes the value.

```
var myInt : Int? = nil
```

Here myInt is declared as an optional of type Int and assigned nil value as the initial value. If you have a valid value, you can simply assign the value to the variable:

```
myInt = 5
```

Now myInt has a valid value of 5, but if you try to use it in an expression, you'll get an error. You have to unbox the optional value before using it. There are two ways to unbox those values:

```
if myInt != nil {
    print(myInt!)
}
```

This uses the ! operator (forced unboxing operator) to access the actual value myInt, telling the runtime I know the variable contains a valid value and I would like to use it. If you try to use the forced unboxing operator when the variable is nil, that will cause an error at runtime.

The second way is using the if let statement:

```
if let tmpInt = myInt {
    print(tmpInt)
}
```

This is a shortcut for checking whether a variable is not nil and unboxing the value. It assigns a valid value to tmpInt (which is not optional), and now you can use the tmpInt within the if statement

You can also use the guard statement; in the previous method the unboxed value can only be used with the if block. With guard statement you unbox the valid value and let the execution continue or fail and execute the guard statements

```
func doubleValue(value : Int?) -> Int? {
    guard let validValue = value else {
        print("the value is nil")
        return nil
    }
    return 2 * validValue
}
```

The above function takes an optional integer and returns the double its value. We unbox the value using the guard statement; if the value is nil we go into the else clause and return nil and exit. If the value is valid then we continue and use the in the rest of the function

Summary

These are the basic building blocks (no pun intended) of your programs, along with control structure statements. Every programming language needs these to program efficiently. Pay close attention to the mutability of the objects. Depending on how you declare your variables, they will impact the performance of your program.

We also introduced the powerful concept of optionals, which will help make your programs safe. You don't want to use optionals all the time, but they can be useful when you're not sure a variable will have a valid value.

Chapter 5

Expressions

Expressions are the building blocks of any program. Values, variables, constants, and functions are combined to form expressions, which, in turn, are combined to form a program. When the program is executed, expressions are interpreted according to the rules set by the particular language. These rules can include precedence and associativity, and they produce results and possibly a new state for the program.

Swift is no different. It provides four types of expressions:

- Primary
- Prefix
- Binary
- Postfix

Evaluating expressions in Swift produces a result, a side effect, or both. There are some expressions that require more information. We will take a look at these and expand on their features and requirements.

> **Note** An expression is said to have a side effect if it modifies some state or has an observable interaction beyond the value of the expression.

Primary Expressions

Primary expressions are the simplest of the expressions. They provide access to values such as x, "This", 4.5, and so forth. These expressions are used in combination with operators to form compound expressions. Some are literal expressions, such as a string literal or a number literal. Other literal expressions are dictionaries and arrays, and the following built-in literals:

- __FILE__ is the name of the file that uses it, and it's a string.
- __LINE__ is the number of the line where it appears, and it's an Int.
- __COLUMN__is the number of the column where it appears, and it's an Int.
- __FUNCTION__ is the name of the declaration in which it's used, and it's a String.

Prefix Expressions

A prefix expression, as the name implies, adds an operator to the beginning of a given expression. Prefix operators take one argument and have the general form:

```
prefix-operator right-hand-side

++index
-5
+192.983
```

Try Operator

The latest release of the language introduces a try operator. The try operator is applied to an expression that can produce and error. The general form is:

```
try expression
```

There is also an *optional-try* expression which when executed; if the error producing expression produces an error the value of the `try`? result is `nil` other wise the valid result from the expression is produced

```
var myResult = try? someErrorProducingFuction()
```

The value of `myResult` will be an optional value if the function does not produce any error, the result of the function will be assigned to `myResult`. If the function produces an error then `nil` value will be assigned.

The third variant of the try expression is a *forced-try* expression which has the same effect as force unboxing.

```
try! someErrorProducingFunction()
```

If the function does not produce an error then the value of the result from function is returned if the function produces and error then there is a runtime error and may cuase a crash in your code.

When the try operator is applied it applies a the who exression to it right side if there is a complex exession then it applies the who expression.

```
try someErrorProducingFunction + someOtherErrorProducingFuction()
```

In this case the scope of the try is both functions is similar to writing

```
(try someErrorProducingFunction + someOtherErrorProducingFuction())
```

If you want reduce the scope and apply to the first fuction then we would write it as

```
(try someErrorProducingFunction() ) + someOtherErrorProducingFunction()
```

Try Does not apply to anything to the left hand side of the expression, except when taking the result from the try.

Postfix Expressions

A postfix expression is where the operator is at the end. In Swift you have two-postfix expression:

- ++ increment
- -- decrement

To use thse you simply add them at the end of the number. `3++` or `3–`

> **Note** Technically, all primary expression are also postfix expressions.

Binary Expressions

Binary expressions are the most common expressions in most languages. They take an argument on the left-hand side (lhs), then an infix operator, and another argument on the right-hand side (rhs). The arguments can be either an expression or an instance of a type, depending on the operator.

```
left-hand-side infix-operator right-hand-side
```

Swift provides a very rich set of binary operators, the most common of these binary expression is the assignment expression using the = operator.

Assignment Operator

The general form of the assignment operator is:

```
left-hand-side = right-hand-side
```

The left hand side is an expression that will be assigned the value(s) from the right hand side expression. The lhs can be a simple value or a compound, such as a structure, a tuple, or an enumeration type. What's new in Swift is the tuple assignment—you can assign multiple values using a tuple. The one requirement is that the lhs tuple and the rhs tuple have the same structure. Here are some valid tuple assignments:

```
(a, b) = (4, 6.5)
(lastName, firstName, middleName) = ("Babbage", "Charles", nil)
(a, _, b, (c, d), x) = (5.0, "Hello", (6, "yellow"), "Apple")
```

If you want to ignore a value during an assignment, use the _ (underscore) in place of that part of the expression. In the third example, the value "Hello" is being ignored during the assignment.

Here are some invalid tuple assignments:

```
(a, b)= 5
(a, b) = (5)
(a, (b, c)) = (1, 2, 3)
```

Ternary Conditional

There's another infix operator that's not binary. It's called the ternary conditional operator and it requires three items. The operator looks like this `?:` and works like an if-else statement but condensed to one line.

```
if condition {
        evaluate true
} else {
        evaluate false
}
```

With the ternary operator, you can rewrite that code as:

```
condition ? evaluate true : evaluate false
```

If-else statements don't return a value, but the ternary operation returns the value of the expression evaluated.

Casting Operators

Swift provides three operators to use when downcasting or introspection types.

- `is`, to check if the type is of a specific type.
- `as`, to downcast the type to another type.
- `as?`, to downcast as an optional type.
- `as!`, to downcase an a forced unboxed type.

To check whether a type can be converted, simply use *expression* `is` *type*. The expression will return true if the expression evaluates to type, or false if expression doesn't evaluate to type.

The general form of these expressions is:

- Expression `is` Type
- Expression `as` Type
- Expression `as?` Type
- Expression `as!` Type

To actually downcast the value, you can use `as`, `as? or as!`. The first one is if the type is known at the compile time and known that will always succeed. With the second, if the downcast succeeds, it's wrapped in an optional. If it fails, the value is `nil`. The last one is forced cast if the cast fails then there is a runtime error, otherwise the valid valid is assigned.

If the compiler knows at compile time that a type can't be cast, that results in a compile-time error. In Cocoa Touch frameworks you can always downcast to `NSObject` because all objects have the same root class. But in Swift, that's not the case, so if the class is not a subclass of another, casting isn't possible and the compiler will give an error.

Self and Super

There are two special expression types called `self` and `super`.

If used within the class function, the `self` expression refers to the type itself, but in an instance method it refers to a specific instance of that type. `Self` can be used in various forms:

```
self.type-member
self[subscript-index]
self(initializer-arguments)
self.init(initializer-arguments)
```

One special case is in mutating structures where you can assign a new value to `self`.

Super is used when referring to a superclass. If the type has a superclass, the form is as follows:

```
super.type-member
super[subscript-index]
super.init(initlizer-arguments)
```

You can also use self as a postfix expression to get the name of the type.

```
expression.self
type.self
```

The first example returns the instance of the expression: A.self just refers to a. The second one returns the type.

Closures and Functions

You already know that functions are just named closures, but the syntax is different and takes getting used to.

Closures

There are various ways the clousers are used in the swift and can be declared in various formats. Since the closures are first class citizens, you can create variables and then pass that variable around the program, to declare a closure as a variable

```
var myClosureVariable : (parameters) -> (returnType)
```

It is similar to defining a variable such as var x : Int, we have not assigned any value to it, they variable can be optional or unboxed optional

```
var myClosureVaraible : (string : String?) -> (String)
var myClosureVaraible2 : ((string : String?) -> (String))?
var myClosureVariable3 : ((string : String?) -> (String))!
```

All of the above variables of the the same type because they take same argument type and return the same type we can now defined an alias for this clouse and use that instead of typing the arguments and return types everytime, use the keyword typealias newType = exitingType

```
typealias MyClosureType = (string : String?) -> (String)
```

Now we can use this new type to define variables

```
var myClosureVaraible4 : MyClosureType
```

Now that you have a variable defined lets assign an actual value to this variable. The general syntax is:

```
{[captured variables] (closure arguments) -> return-type in
        closure-body
}

myClosureVaraible4 = { (string : String?) -> String in
    return string ?? ""
}
```

If you don't have arguments or a return type, these can be inferred. There are special forms of closures. Here are rules you can apply to make your closure as verbose or terse as you'd like.

- A closure can omit the types of its arguments.
- A closure can omit its return type.
- If you omit both the argument types and names, omit the in keyword before the statements.
- If you omit the argument list, the arguments are explicitly named $0, $1, ...
- If the closure has only a single expression in the body, this implies that the closure returns the value of the expression; the return statement can be omitted.

Here are some examples; these are all equivalent:

```
{ (a : Int, b : Int) -> Int in
    return a % b
}

{ (a, b) in
    return a % b
}

{ return $0 % %1 }

{ $0 % %1 }
```

If you use a reference type within the closure, you'll be capturing the variable strongly, as discussed in Chapter 14.

If you specify a capture list, you have to specify the in keyword in the closure.

```
{ self.type-member } // strong reference to self
{ [weak self] in self!.type-member } // weak reference to self
{ [unowned self] in self.type-member } // unowned reference
{ [weak weakSelf = self] in weakSelf!.type-member }
```

Function Calls

To call a function, the syntax is the name of the function followed by a list of arguments in parentheses separated by commas:

```
function-name(argument1, argument2)
```

If the function call requires argument names, you add the argument names before each argument, separated by a colon:

```
function-name(argumentName1 : argument1, argumentName2 : argument2)
```

There's a special case where, if the function has a trailing closure (a final argument is a closure), you can move the closure out from the argument list and add it to the end of the function call:

```
function-name(argument1, {closure})
function-name(argument1) {closure}
```

Both of these statements are equivalent. If the closure is the only argument, you can even skip the parentheses

```
Function-name({closure})
Function-name{closure}
```

There's also a special initializer function called `init`:

```
expression.init(argument-list)
```

You can't use the `init` functions to initialize variables since they don't return any value:

```
var result = type.classFunction //correct
var result = type.init // error
```

Implicit Member Expression

In previous examples we used explicit .type-member expressions. When the type can be inferred, you can use an abbreviated form for enumeration cases or class methods. Inside the classes you don't need the dot syntax to access methods, initializers, and so forth. The only time you have to be explicit is when the name of an argument to a method is the same as the property name.

```
var domainMask : NSSearchPathDomainMask = .UserDomainMask
```

With explicit member expression, in contrast, you explicitly access the value:

```
var instance = SomeClass()
instance.member-item
```

For tuples, the member items are accessed by numeric dereference:

```
var myTuple = (a, b, c, d)
myTuple.1 // returns b
```

Optionals

One of the features of Swift is the optional type. When you declare an optional variable, you are telling the compiler that this variable might or might not have a value. To get a valid value from an optional is called *unwrapping* the optional.

If you know that the value of an optional is not nil, you can forceably unwrap using the ! (bang) operator. If the value that's unwrapped is not a valid value, you will get a runtime error.

```
var a : Int? = 0
var b : Int = 5
a! += b
```

The result of an optional expression is always an optional type

```
expression?
```

This expression returns the value as an optional. The way it works is that if the optional unwraps as a valid value, the rest of the expression is evaluated and the result is returned, otherwise nil is returned.

```
class SomeClass {
        func someFunction() -> Int {
                return 42
        }
}

var someInstance : Int?
var result = someInstance?.someFunction()
```

The type of the result is `Int?` because even though the return type of `someFunction` is `Int`, `someInstance` is an optional. If `someInstance` exists, the result will have the value `42`; if `someInstance` is `nil` then result will be `nil`.

There is another way to optionally unwrap an optional using the `if-let` expression.

```
if let unwrapped = someInstance {
        result = unwrapped.someFunction()
}
```

In this case, if `someInstance` has a valid value, it is assigned to `unwrapped` and then the `if` statement is evaluated to be true and the statements in the `if` statement are executed, otherwise the condition for the `if` statement is evaluated to be false and it's skipped.

Optional Chainning

Optional chainning is another operator ?? (two questions together) where you give a list of the exrepssions that return optional value of the same type, then first expression that returns a valid valid it is used. The simplist form is two expressions separated by ??

```
exrepssion1 ?? expression2
```

if the expression1 has a valid value then expression2 is ignored and value return from expression1 is used. You can chain multiple of these together

```
expression1 ?? expression2 ?? expression3 ?? "Valid String"
```

In the above example all expression must return a string type, if none of them return a valid string value then the `"Valid String"` is returned.

Summary

This was a quick overview of expressions; there's a lot more to learn and experiment with. You'll be using most if not all of these expressions in your programs. You learned about optionals, and optional chaining how it can help you write safer code.

Chapter 6

Operators

General-purpose languages provide set of operators—convenience constructs that behave like functions—and Swift is no different. You've already seen at least one such operator: +. Swift provides a wide range of built-in operators and allows you to define operators for your own classes and to extend built-in classes to add new operators.

Syntax

Operators in Swift can be:

- Unary, which requires only one operand or input. (-a).
- Binary, which requires two operands or inputs. (a+b).
- Ternary, which requires three operands. (?:).

Notation

Operators come in one of three notations:

- Prefix, where the operator comes before the operand(s). The operator can be either unary or binary. (++a)
- Infix, where the operator requires two operands and comes between them. (a + b)
- Postfix, where the operand(s) come before the operator. The operator can be unary or binary. (a++)

Precedence

Precedence specifies the order in which operators are applied to values in complex expressions. Higher-precedence operators are given higher priority and are evaluated before those with lower precedence. As you know, multiplication has higher precedence than addition. Suppose you have the expression 1 + 2 * 3. If there were no operator precedence, there'd be two options for evaluating and, depending on which you chose, (1 + 2) * 3 or 1 + (2 * 3), you'd get either 9 or 7. Instead, because multiplication has higher precedence, the answer is always 7 because the multiplication operator is applied to its operands before the addition is. Of course, you can change this binding by using parentheses to set the order. In Swift, precedence is defined by an integer; higher values have higher precedence. Built-in operators have a defined precedence. Overloaded operator precedence is defined in the declaration.

Associativity

If a statement contains operators with the same precedence, how is that resolved? Look at the expression 1 – 2 + 3. Since both the + and – have the same precedence, you could evaluate this to either 2 or -4, depending on which side you start to evaluate the expression. If we start to evaluate the expression from the left we would have 1 – 2 followed by + 3, and if we were to start evaluating from the right side then we would have 3+2 and then followed by subtracting the result from 1.

In Swift, mathematical operators have left associativity, meaning that evaluation starts from the left and goes to the right, so that statement is always evaluated as ((1 – 2) + 3).

Swift Operators

Now let's look at the Swift operators, starting with the prefixes, then the infix operators, and finally the postfix operators.

Prefix

- + Unary Plus, +4
- - Unary Minus, -5
- ++ Increment, ++i
- -- Decrement, --i
- ! Logical NOT, !expression (the expression must evaluate to a Bool)
- ~ Bitwise NOT, ~expression (the expression must evaluate to a number)

Infix

As we discussed in Chapter 5, the infix operators require two operands with left-hand side expression and right-hand side expression. Here are the infix operators in order of decreasing precedence.

Bitwise Shift (precedence 160)

Integers are represented bitwise shift operatoras bits. As you know, Int8 is eight bits, so to store 5 you'd have 00000101. If you shift the bits left by 1 bit, you get 00001010, and if you shift the original 00000101 by 1 bit to the right, you have 00000010.

- The left-shift operator is <<. To left-shift a number *n* by *m* bits, you write `n << m`.
- The right-shift operator is >>. To right-shift a number *n* by *m* bits, you write `n >> m`.

With unsigned integers, the bit-shifting behavior is as follows:

- Existing bits are moved to the left or right by the requested number of places.
- Any bits that are moved beyond the bounds of the integer's storage are discarded.
- Zeroes are inserted in the spaces left behind after the original bits are moved to the left or right.

The following illustrates shifting an unsigned integer to the left 1 bit:

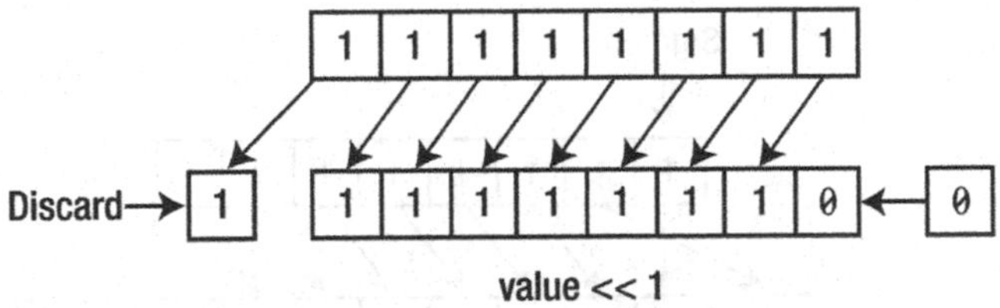

Unsigned Shift Left

The following illustrates shifting an unsigned integer to the right 1 bit:

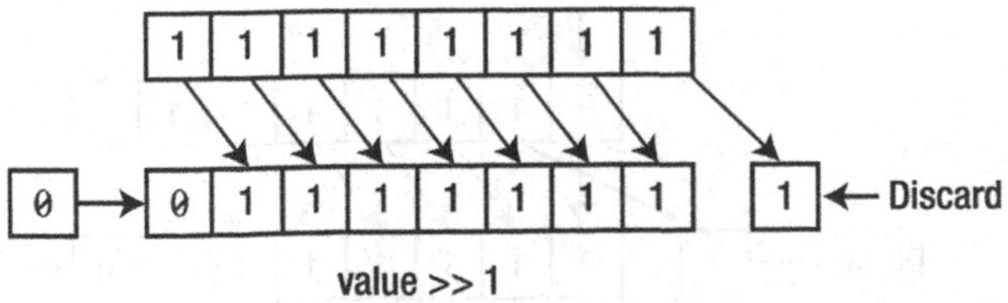

Unsigned Shift Right

And this shows the results of some left and right shifts:

```
let value: UInt8 = 4    // 00000100 in binary
value << 1              // 00001000
value << 2              // 00010000
value << 5              // 10000000
value << 6              // 00000000
value >> 2              // 00000001
```

Signed integers require an extra bit to denote the + or – sign. The first bit reading from left to right (the most significant bit) is used for that purpose; the value 0 indicates a positive number and 1 a negative number. Examples here will use 8-bit numbers, but the principles apply to larger numbers as well.

Negative numbers are stored in 2's complement format, which means you subtract the absolute value from 2 to the power of the number of value bits. For 8-bit numbers, the number of value bits is 7, and 2^7 = 128.

This example represents 4 as a signed integer, first positive and then negative: 128 – 4 = 124.

```
let value : Int8 = 4  // 00000100
let value : Int8 = -4 // 11111100
```

The bit-shifting behavior for signed integers is as follows:

- Shifting left is the same as for unsigned numbers.
- Shifting right is the same as for unsigned numbers, but the new signed bit is the same as the previous value to ensure the number keeps its sign.

This illustrates shifting a signed integer with a negative value 1 bit left:

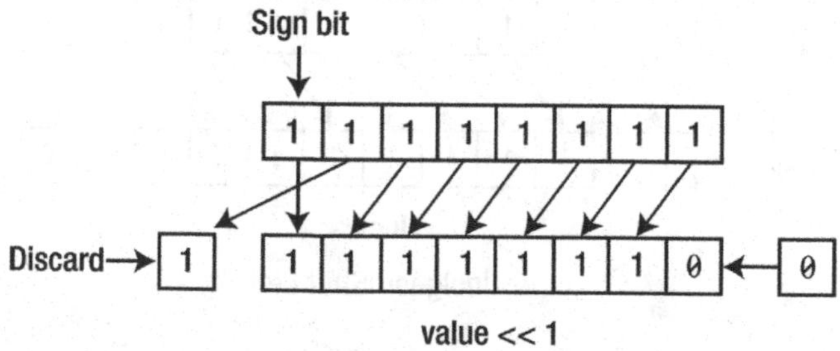

Signed Shift Left Negative Value

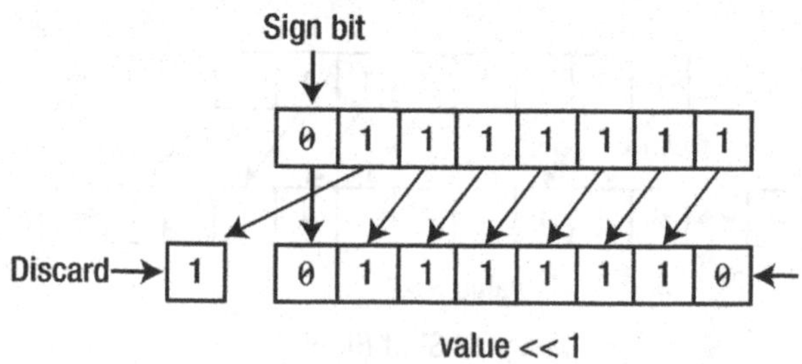

Signed Shift Left Positive Value

This illustrates shifting a signed integer with a negative value right 1 bit:

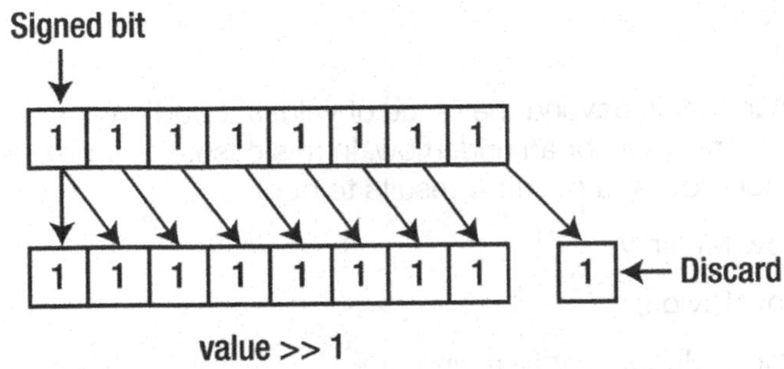

Signed Shift Right Negative Value

This illustrates shifting a signed integer with a positive value right 1 bit:

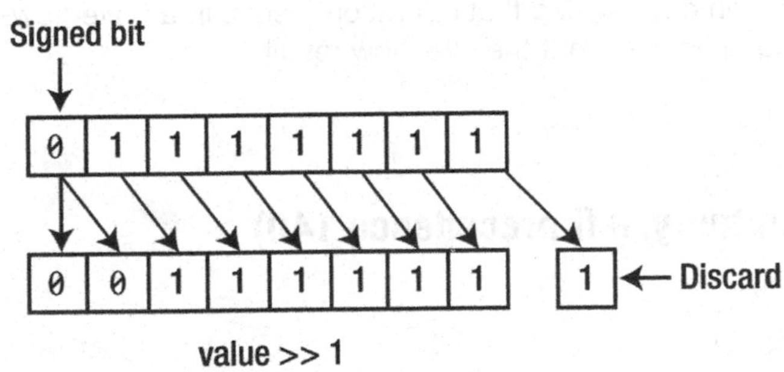

Signed Shift Right Positive Value

Here are some examples:

```
let value: Int8 = -4  // 11111100 in binary
value << 1             // 11111000
value << 2             // 11110000
value << 5             // 10000000
value << 6             // 00000000
value >> 2             // 11111111
```

Multiplicative (associativity left, precedence 150)

- * (Multiply)
- / (Divide)
- % (Modulus or Remainder)
- & (Bitwise AND)

```
let a = 5 * 8
let b = 6 / 4
let c = 6 % 4
let d = 6 & 4
```

If you are using a value that is beyond the range of values a particular type can hold, that value will cause an overflow or an underflow. In this case, you must use the special operators to allow underflow and overflow results to occur:

- &* (Overflow Multiply)
- &/ (Overflow Divide)
- &% (Overflow Modulus or Remainder)

Let's try this code:

```
let e : Int8 = 127 * 2
```

The compiler gives us an error saying that operation results in an overflow, we must use the overflow to tell the compiler we want the over flow result.

```
let e : Int8 = 127 &* 2
```

Additive (associativity, left precedence 140)

- + (Addition)
- - (Subtraction)
- &+ (Overflow Addition)
- &- (Overflow Subtraction)
- | (Bitwise AND)
- ^ (Bitwise XOR)

```
let f = a + b
let g = a - b

let h : Int8 = 127 &+ 50

let j = 6 | 4
let k = 6 ^ 4
```

Range (precedence 135)

Rangeoperators define a range of values, and Swift has two types of range operators:

- ..< (Half-Open Range)
- ... (Closed Range)

To count all of the numbers in a range, including the first and last ones, use the closed-range operator. If you don't want to include the final value, use the half-open operator. So if you want to include 10 in the range from 1 to 10, you'd use the closed-range operator, but if you want to include all the numbers through 9 but not including 10, you'd use the half-open operator.

```
for i in 1..<10 {
    print(i)
}
// prints 1 2 3 4 5 6 7 8 9
for i in 1...10 {
    print(i)
}
// prints 1 2 3 4 5 6 7 8 9 10
```

Cast (precedence 132)

When you convert one object type to another it's called casting. Swift provides two operators: the is operator to check whether the object can be cast to the indicated type, and the as operator to actually cast the value.

```
class Fruit {
}

class Banana : Fruit {
}

var fruit : Fruit = Banana()
if fruit is Banana {
    var banana = fruit as! Banana
}
var anotherFruit = Fruit()
if anotherFruit is Banana {
    var banana = anotherFruit as! Banana
}
var possibleBanana = fruit as? Banana
var notBanana = anotherFruit as? Banana
```

The first example shows two types: a parent type called `Fruit` and a subtype called `Banana`. First we create a variable called `fruit` of the explicit type `Fruit`, and then we initialize it with type `Banana`, since banana is also of type `Fruit`. Next we check to see if the type can be cast using the is operator. The statement `fruit is Banana` will evaluate to true and we can have our `Banana`.

In the second example, `anotherFruit` can't be converted to `Banana` since we initialized it as `Fruit`.

Comparative (precedence 130)

You've already seen most of these operators in other languages and they're fairly self-explanatory. But Swift provides some additional ones.

- < (Less Than)
- <= (Less Than or Equal)
- > (Greater Than)
- >= (Greater Than or Equal)
- == (Equal To)
- != (Not Equal To)
- === (Identical)
- !== (Not Identical)
- ~= (Pattern Match)

When working with reference types, two objects can sometimes point to a single instance of an object. The Swift equal to operator (==) checks the values of the objects. To check whether the two variables or constants point to the same instance of an object, you use the identity operator (===).

```
if banana === fruit {
    print("they are the same")
}
// prints “they are the same”

if banana !== anotherFruit {
    print("they are not the same")
}
// does "they are not the same"
```

Conjunctive (associativity, left precedence 120)

- && (Logical AND)

Disjunctive (associativity, left precedence 110)

- || (Logical OR)

Nil Coalescing (associativity, right precedence 110)

- ?? (Nil Coalescing)

In Chapter 5 we talked about optional types and how to box and unbox them. The nil coalescing operator can help you write less code when unboxing optional types.

```
var variable1 : String? = nil
var variable2 : String? = "Hello"
var value = variable1 ?? variable2
```

In this example there are two optional variables: `variable1` and `variable2`. One has a valid value and the other doesn't. If we were writing this using `if` statements, we would check whether `variable1` has a valid value and, if so, use that value. Otherwise we would use the `variable2` value. Suppose `variable2` does not have a valid value either and we wanted to assign it some default value to the variable `value`. In a typical if-else statement we would write this as

```
if variable1 != nil {
    value = variable1
} else if variable2 != nil {
    value = variable2
} else {
    value = "Unknown Value"
}
```

In Swift we can use the Nil Coalescing operator and we can write it very concisely

```
var value = variable1 ?? variable2 ?? "Unknown Value"
```

This is a trivial example and you could probably write a simple if/else statement. But what if you had a bunch of variables you wanted to get the value from? You could do so simply, like this:

```
var value = var1 ?? var2 ?? var3 ?? var4 ?? var5 ?? “Default Value”
```

The code reads as if `var1` has a value assigned to it. If it doesn't, the code checks whether `var2` has a value assigned to it, and so on until the last, which in this case is "`Default Value`." The value of the first variable reached that has a valid value will be assigned to `value`.

Ternary Conditional (associativity, right precedence 100)

- ?: (If-Then-Else Conditional)

```
var result : Int
if a == 10 {
    result = a
} else {
    result = b
}

var result = a == 10 ? a : b
```

Assignment (associativity, right precedence 90)

- = (Assign)
- *= (Multiply and Assign)
- /= (Divide and Assign)
- %= (Modulus and Assign)
- += (Addition and Assign)
- -= (Subtraction and Assign)
- <<= (Left bitshift and Assign)
- >>= (Right bitshift and Assign)
- &= (Bitwise AND and Assign)
- ^= (Bitwise XOR and Assign)
- |= (Bitwise OR and Assign)
- &&= (Logical AND and Assign)
- ||= (Logical OR and Assign)

Postfix

- value++ (Increment)
- value-- (Decrement)

Overloading Operators

Swift lets you use existing operators with your custom types or additional built-in types. To overload an existing operator, you define a function that takes the appropriate number of arguments and types for which the operator is overloaded. This is a controversial topic that leads to confusion and ambiguity, and that's bad for programming, which needs to always get the exact same result for the same set of inputs and operations.

Let's say you want to add a string and a number, but what would the end result be? If you wrote the expression `"Hello" + 12`, what should it produce? Should something like this even be allowed? So think carefully before you start to experiment with operator overloading. Here are some guidelines to help you decide:

- Don't create an operator unless the meaning is clear.
- Operators should be created for convenience. The functionality should be implemented in a separate function that the operator function uses.
- Be sure to provide proper precedence and associativity. Try matching the existing operator as closely as possible.
- You may also want to create assignment operators if necessary.

Unary Operator

With all that said, let's create an operator, the mathematical symbol ∑, which will be used to sum all numbers in an array. It will be a unary prefix operator and will be written as follows:

> **Note** To type ∑ symbol on an OS X system you use the ⌥ (Option, Alt) key and the W key together.

```
var a = [Double] = [30.04, 95.3, 12.9, 0.01, 0.0]
let b = Σa
let b = Σ[30.04, 95.3, 12.9, 0.01, 0.0]
```

Since this is a unary operator, I don't need to worry about precedence and associativity. Creating the new operator is a two-step process: First we declare that it's an operator and then we actually implement the function for it.

```
prefix operator Σ {}
```

- The `prefix` keyword specifies the type of operator (must be `prefix`, `infix`, or `postfix`).
- The `operator` reserved keyword indicates it's an operator.
- Σ is the operator itself.
- The braces {} are where you can specify precedence and associativity for infix operators.

Next we define the function that actually does the work. Since this is a `prefix` operator, we start with that keyword, followed by the reserved keyword `func` and then the operator name.

The next steps are to set the kind of arguments the function takes and the kind of value(s) the function returns, and then finally to write the body of the function.

```
prefix operator Σ {}
prefix func Σ (array : [Double]) -> Double {
    return array.reduce(0, combine: {(a, b) -> Double in
        return a + b
    })
}
```

If we really wanted to be concise using the closure rules, we can rewrite the implementation as

```
prefix operator Σ {}
prefix func Σ (array : [Double]) -> Double {
    return array.reduce(0) {$0 + $1}
}

let b = Σ[1.0, 2.0, 3.0] // b = 6.0
let a = [4.0, 5.0, 6.0, 7.0]
let c = Σa // c = 22.0
```

So what happens when the sum overflows? As you know, Swift will mark it as an error, so you should also provide a ∑& operator to handle the overflow conditions.

Binary Operators

There are plenty of binary operators to choose from: ×, ÷, ±, and so on. No doubt you learned as a child that ÷ is divide, so we are going to make that the new operator.

```
infix operator ÷ { associativity left precedence 150}
func ÷ (left : Double, right : Double) -> Double {
    return left / right
}

let d = 200.0 ÷ 2 // d = 100.0
```

But if we do that, we get:

```
var e = 10.0
e ÷= 2
```

We get an error, because we haven't created a ÷= operator. Now let's do that.

```
infix operator ÷= {associativity right precedence 90}
func ÷= (inout left : Double, right : Double) {
    left = left ÷ right
}
```

Left is marked as `inout` because we need to update the value and send it back to the calling function. We are not done yet—what happens if we divide the left by the value 0? Well, now we have to make the overflow operator ÷&. As you can see, that operator rabbit hole is quite deep, so you need to think carefully about all potential scenarios and make operators that cover most cases.

Summary

These operators come with the Swift standard library. You are probably familiar with most of them from your math classes or from other programming languages. You'll end up using most of them, if not all, in your programs. When you're creating your own types, you'll probably need some custom operators to help make your types concise and easy to work with.

Sometimes you might want to extend an existing type to provide new operators for convenience, and Swift provides an easy way to do so. When creating your own operators, be careful of the operators that are built into the standard library or the types.

Also keep in mind that when defining custom operators you should follow the well-known conventions and meanings of the operator. Don't define - operator to do addition or + to do division. If you do that, developers will not end up using your types.

Chapter 7

Flow Control

In programming, Control Flow refers to how the order of instructions (statements) are executed. Swift provides the standard set of conditional constructs. These include `for`, `repeat`, `while`, `if`, `do`, `guard`, and `switch`, plus break and continue to transfer the control to another location in the code.

Even though these constructs are familiar, they provide considerably powerful support for safety.

For Loops

A *for* loop construct provides a way for a block of code to be executed a number of times. Swift provides two types of `for` loops.

- `For-in` is used in conjunction with objects that are contained in a range, sequence, collection, or progression. These typically include arrays and dictionaries.
- For-conditional-increment performs a block of code until the fail condition is met; usually the fail condition is dependent on a counter.

For-in

You can use the `for-in` loop to iterate over collections (arrays, dictionaries, strings, etc).

Let's start with something simple. We have a range of values that we iterate.

```
for i in 1...6 {
   print(i)
}
```

The above code will print numbers from 1 to 6. The range operator three dots (...) is called a closed range operator, which means that the loop will execute from 1 to 6 inclusive. The value of i is set to first index, which in this case is 1, and then the block of code within the curly braces is executed. When the statements in the block are finished, the value of i is updated to the next value in the range, in this case 2, and the block is executed again. This process happens repeatedly until the end of the range is reached.

Things to notice

- The value i does not need to be declared before it can be used in the for loop.
- i is declared constant for each iteration as if declared with the let keyword.
- The value of i is only available within the loop block.

We did not specify the type for i by default; it will be inferred to be the Int type. If you would like to use another int type such as Int8 or Int16, simply specify like you would when declaring a variable.

```
for i : Int8 in 1...6 {
    print(i)
}
```

> **Note** Keep in mind that if the range overflows the type, then that is an error and Swift will mark it as such.

If you would like to access the value of i outside the loop, then you have to declare it before the loop as a var, and then you can modify within the loop and have access outside.

```
var i = -1
for j in 1... 6 {
      i = j
}
print(i)   // prints 6
```

If you do not need the individual values of the range and would like to ignore them, then you can use the underscore _ instead of the variable.

```
for _ in 1...6 {
    var a = arc4random() % 3
    print(a)
}
```

In languages where arrays are zero based, the index of the first element is 0, so the range is from 0 to n-1 for an array of n elements. To support this, Swift provides a half-closed range operator ..<. In this case the last value in the range is not included.

```
for i in 1..<6 {
    print(i)
}
```

This will only print values from 1 to 5.

As we discussed in an earlier chapter, the curly braces are required for the `for` loop. This is different from Objective-C where for a single statement curly braces were optional.

This loop construct comes handy with collections.

```
let animals = ["Dog", "Cat", "Fish", "Lion"]
for animal in animals {
    print(animal)
}
```

For dictionaries, you can use the tuples as the constant values returned from dictionary. Each tuple is a key/value pair (key, value), and we can decompose the tuple to use the explicitly named constants that can be used within the body of the loop.

```
let numberOfWheels = ["car" : 4, "bicycle" : 2, "tricycle" : 3]
for (mode, wheelCount) in numberOfWheels {
    print("The \(mode) has \(wheelCount) wheels")
}
```

In this example we decompose the keys as `mode` and values as `wheelCount` constants in the loop.

The items in the dictionaries may not necessarily be iterated in the order they were inserted. The contents of the dictionaries depend on the keys, and they are inherently unordered. So the order is not guaranteed.

You can also use the `for-in` loop for strings. Strings are just an ordered collection of characters.

```
for character in "Adam".characters{
    print(character)
}
```

For-conditional-Increment

This is the traditional C style `for` loop. It has general the format

```
for initialization; condition; increment {
    statements
}
for var i = 1; i <= 6; i++ {
    print(i)
}
```

The loop execution follows:

1. When the loop is first entered the initialization statement is evaluated.
2. The conditional is evaluated; if the conditional evaluates to false, the loop ends and the block is not executed and the program continues after the closing curly brace. If the conditional expression evaluated to true, then the block is executed.
3. After the block has executed the increment part is evaluated. After that the execution of the program goes back to step 2 and the condition expression is evaluated again.

```
var i = 1
for ; i <= 6; i++ {
    print(i)
}

var i = 1
for ; i <= 6; {
    print(i)
    i++
}
```

Both of the above do the same thing. If you declare the variable as part of the initialization expression such as var i = 0, those variables are only available with the body of the loop; if you need to access those values outside the loop, they must be declared outside the for statement.

```
var i : Int
for i = 1; i <= 6; i++ {
    print(i)
}
print(i)
```

While

The `while` loop has two parts: the condition and the statements. The `while` loop evaluates the condition, and if the condition is `true` the statements are executed. This is repeated until the condition evaluates to `false`, and then the execution of the program continues after the closing curly brace.

```
while condition {
  statements
}
var n = 3456, s = 0, d = 0
```

```
while n != 0 {
    d = n % 10
    s = s * 10 + d
    n = n / 10
}
print(s) // 6543
```

Repeat-while

In `repeat-while` loop the condition is at the end of the loop. That means that statements are executed at least once. The general form is

```
repeat {
  statements
} while condition
```

```
var a = 2, r = 0, n = 45
repeat {
    r = n % a
    if r == 0 {
        print(a) // 3, 5, 9, 15
    }
    a++
} while a <= n/2
```

Branch Statements

During the execution of your program you need to make choices as to which piece of code needs to execute depending on a condition. You call that conditional code. Swift provides you with two ways to handle conditional code, using either the `if` statement or a `switch` statement. `If` is useful when you have a limited number of permutations of the conditions. `Switch` is suited for more complex situations.

`If`, in its simplest form, puts a guard around statements with a condition and only execute those statements if the condition is true. The parentheses around the condition are not required. The curly braces around the statements are required even if there is only one statement.

```
if condition {
   statements
}
```

> **Note** In C the condition only needs to be nonzero value, and it would be considered true. Not in Swift: the condition must evaluate to a Bool type.

```
let a = 10, b = 20
if a < b {
    print("a is smaller than b")
}
```

The code above checks if a is less then b, which in this case is true and evaluates to true and the message is printed. If the condition evaluates to false then the message is not printed. The execution continues after the closing curly brace of the `if` statement.

`If` also provides an alternative statement if the condition is not true.

```
if condition {
   statements1
} else {
   statements2
}
```

In this case one of the two sets of statements is executed. If the condition is true `statements1` are executed; if the condition is false then the `statements2` are executed. The execution continues after the last closing brace of the `if` statement.

```
let a = 20, b = 10

if a < b {
    print("a is smaller than b")
} else {
    print("a is larger than b")
}
```

You can have zero or more `else if` .conditions. The last else is not required if not needed.

```
if condition1 {
   statements1
} else if condition2 {
   statements2
} else {
  statements3
}

let a = 10, b = 20, c = 30

if a > b && a > c {
   print("a is the greatest")
} else if b > c {
   print("b is the greatest")
} else {
   print("c is the greatest")
}
```

A guard statement is similar to an `if` statement where the conditional must be met before the execution can continue. A `guard` statement differs from `if` statement in that `guard` always has an `else` statement; if the condition is not met the else block is executed.

```
func hello(person : String?) {
    guard let name = person else {
        print("Hello")
        return
    }

    print("Hello " + name)
}
hello(nil)
hello("Waqar")
```

This function checks the input if we have a valid name, then we continue and print the hello message with the name. Otherwise we just print hello.

Switch

Sometimes you want to execute .one of many different sequences of statements based on the value of a single expression. You can do this by using a set of `else if` statements, but most languages (including Swift) provide a simpler way to do this.

Swift's mechanism is a `switch` statement. The `switch` statement computes the value of an expression, and then compares it to lists of values to determine what to execute next. The general form is

```
switch condition {
  case value1:
        statements for value1
  case value2:
        statements for value2
  default:
        statements for othervalues
}
```

To match a value it must placed after the `case` keyword. Every switch statement must be exhaustive; that is, every possible value must be considered. Let's say if you are matching against integer values, it is not possible to match every last integer. You can specify a catchall case called the `default`. If none of the cases are matched then the statements in the `default` are executed. The `default` case must appear at the end of the case list.

```
let character : Character = "r"
switch character {
case "a", "e", "i", "o", "u":
    print("A vowel")
default:
    print("Not a vowel")
}
// Not a vowel
```

There is no explicit fallthrough for case statements. Every case must provide at least one executable statement. If you do not have any code to execute or just want to exit the switch statement, use the break statement to leave the switch. The following code will give you can error, because the first four cases do not have any statements (and there is no fallthrough).

```
let character : Character = "r"
switch character {
case "a":
case "e":
case "i":
case "o":
case "u":
    print("A vowel")
default:
    print("Not a vowel")
}
```

If you would like to fall through explicitly, you have to use the keyword fallthrough. The above code can be correctly written as:

```
let character : Character = "a"
switch character {
case "a":
    fallthrough
case "e":
    fallthrough
case "i":
    fallthrough
case "o":
    fallthrough
case "u":
    print("A vowel")
default:
    print("Not a vowel")
}
```

You can also match multiple values in a case by separating them with a comma.

```
let character : Character = "a"
switch character {
case "a", "e", "I", "o", "u":
    print("a vowel")
default:
    print("not a vowel")
}
```

Range Matching

You can also use the range operators in the case statements.

```
let number = 300000
switch number {
case 0 ..< 10:
    print("Units")
case 10 ... 99:
    print("tens")
case 100 ... 999:
    print("Hundreds")
case 1000 ... 999_999:
    print("thousands")
case 1_000_000 ..< 1_000_000_000:
    print("millions")
case 1_000_000_000 ..< 1_000_000_000_000:
    print("billions")
default:
    print("a vary large number")
}
```

Tuples

You use tuplesto test the multiple values in the same switch statement; each element in the tuple can be tested for a different value or range of values. If you would like to match any value in a tuple you can use the _ as the matching parameter.

```
let latlon = (36, -77)
switch latlon {
case (0, -180...180):
     print("On the equator!")
default:
    print("Not on the equator")
}
```

The above case statement will match to make sure that first item in the tuple matches to 0 and the rest of it matches between -180 to 180 for the second value. If the first value does not match then the second value will be ignored.

Value Binding

The switch statement can bind values to temporary constants that can be used within the body of the switch. A case with value binding matches all possible values for that value.

```
let latlon = (36, -77)
switch latlon {
case (0, let lon):
     print("On the equator at longitude \(lon)!")
```

```
case (let lat, let lon):
    print("At latitude \(lat) and longitude \(lon)")
}
```

String Matching

Not only can match individual characters, but can you match strings in the case statement.

```
let carMaker = "Porsche"

switch carMaker {
case "BMW", "Porsche", "Audi", "VW":
    print("German")
case "Toyota", "Nissan", "Mazda":
    print("Japanese")
case "GM", "Ford":
    print("American")
default:
    print("Unknown")
}
```

Where Clause

You can use the where clause in the case expression to check for additional conditions.

```
let fraction = (10, 20)
switch fraction {
case let (num, 0):
     print("dividing by zero")
case let(num, den) where num % den == 0:
     print("the fraction represents a whole numbe \(num/dem)r")
case let (num, den):
     print("non whole number \(num) over \(den)")
}
```

We first decompose the fraction to its individual items in the tuple for each case. The first case we check, if the denominator is a 0 then we get an error. Next we check if the remainder (% operator) is zero; that means the numerator is a multiple of the denominator. The last case matches everything.

```
let vowels : Set<Character> = ["a", "e", "i", "o", "u"]
let consonants : Set<Character> = ["b", "c", "d", "f", "g", "h", "j", "k", "l", "m","n",
"p", "q", "r", "s", "t", "v", "w", "x", "y", "z"]
let character : Character = "r"
switch character {
case let value where vowels.contains(value):
    print("vowel")
case let value where consonants.contains(value):
    print("consonant")
```

```
default:
    print("Not english alphabet")
}
```

The first case clause will match whatever that value the variable `character` has, in our case it is "r", since we added the where clause for membership of the matched character to be in the `vowels` set. In this case since "r" is not in the set and fails the where clause that in turn fails the whole case clause.

Now that our first case clause did not match, we go the next clause we still match the value to "r" and then we evaluate the where clause to check the membership in the `consonants` set. In this case the where clause is true, which causes this clause to be true. Now we print the correct message that "r" is a consonant.

Let's say if the value of `character` was "ä", this is not in either the `consonants` or `vowels` set we will fail the first and the second case clauses, and then we will match the default case.

Control Transfer Statements

When you need to change the order of execution of your program, you can use one of the five statements.`control transfer statements`

Continue

The `continue` statement in the body of the loop tells the loop to skip the rest of the statements in the loop and go to the beginning of the loop.

```
var odds = [Int]()
for i in 1...20 {
    switch i {
    case let a where a % 2 == 0:
        continue
    default:
        odds.append(i)
    }
}

print(odds)
```

We just want to filter out odd numbers from 1 to 20; we use our `switch` statement to test if the number is even. If it is even then we continue to the next iteration of the loop. Any statements after `continue` are skipped over and the execution goes to the top of the loop.

Break

Break statement stops the execution of the entire control flow block. Break statement can be used in loops and switch statements.

When break statement is used within a loop, the execution of the loop stops immediately at the break statement and falls out of the loop, and the execution of the program continues after the closed curly brace (}) of the loop.

```
for i in odds {
    if i == 11 {
        break
    }
    print(i)
}
```

In this simple example we iterate over our odd numbers. We loop over the numbers until we get to 11 and then we are done. As soon as we match 11 we stop the execution of the for loop.

Break statement in switch ends the execution of the switch statement and the execution of the program continues at the closing brace (}). Sometimes it is useful where you don't want to execute a statement after matching a case in the switch statement; in this case you can use the break statement to exit out of the switch statement.

```
enum Suit : Int {
    case Diamonds
    case Hearts
    case Spades
    case Clubs
    case Joker
}

let hand = Suit.Diamonds

switch hand {
case .Diamonds:
    print("Diamonds")
case .Hearts:
    print("Hearts")
case .Spades:
    print("Spades")
case .Clubs:
    print("Clubs")
default:
    print("Joker")
}
```

```
switch hand {
case .Diamonds, .Hearts, .Spades, .Clubs:
    break
default:
    print("joker")
}

switch hand {
case let value where value == .Joker:
    print("Joker")
default:
    break
}
```

Because every case must have at least one executable statement, in our case we did not want to print any message. We just used break statement to exit the switch statement.

Fallthrough

The switch case statements do not fall through to the next case statement. Instead, once the statements in a particular case are executed, the switch statement ends and the flow continues outside of the switch statement. You have to explicitly note that after executing the statements in the current case clause to go to the next case clause (fallthrough) and execute the set of statements for that clause as well.

In C based language it is the opposite; you have to explicitly stop from executing statements from the next case by adding the `break` keyword. You can also add the `break` keyword at the end the statements for each case clause but you are not required. It is only required if it is the only statement, because swift requires that each case clause must have one executable statement.

```
switch hand {
case .Diamonds:
    print"Yippie")
    fallthrough
case .Hearts:
    print("Got Red card")
case .Spades:
    fallthrough
case .Clubs:
    print("Got Black card")
default:
    print("Got Joker")
}
```

In this example we print both “Yippie” and “Got Red Card”

```
switch hand {
case let value where value == .Diamonds || value == .Hearts:
    print("got red card")
case let value where value == .Clubs || value == .Spades:
    print("got black card")
```

```
default:
    print("Joker")
}
```

Return

The return statement is used in functions to end the execution of the function and skip the rest of the statements in the function. A typical scenario is checking if the arguments of the function are valid before continuing with the function.

```
func myfunction(input1 : Int?) {
    if nil == input1 {
        return
    }

    print("We executing function")
}
```

Throw

Throw statement is used when there is an error and we want to return the control flow to calling scope and end the current execution. We will discuss throw and error handling in Chapter 16; in this example our function is marked as causing an error, or returning a valid value. We define our error type, and we throw that error if the input value is nil

```
enum MyErrors : ErrorType {
    case InvalidValue
}

func myFunction(value : Int?) throws -> Int {
    guard let theValue = value else {
        throw MyErrors.InvalidValue
    }
    return 2 * theValue
}

func myFunction2(value : Int?) throws -> Int {
    if let theValue = value {
        return 2 * theValue
    } else {
        throw MyErrors.InvalidValue
    }
}
```

Labeled Statements

You can have nested switch statements and loops; sometimes it is important to explicitly halt or skip a specific loop or switch block. Swift allows you to label loops and switch statements so you can explicitly break or continue a particular loop or switch

```
label-name : while  condition  {
    statements
}
```

Use this label after either break or continue. We can rewrite our earlier for loops.

```
var odds = [Int]()
oddsloop : for i in 1...20 {
    switch i {
    case let a where a % 2 == 0:
        continue oddsloop
    default:
        odds.append(i)
    }
}

oddsloop1 : for i in odds {
    if i == 11 {
        break oddsloop1
    }
    print(i)
}
```

Keep in mind that label is only available in the scope of the loop or switch statement.

Summary

Control flow is what helps users write complex programs. Swift provide a rich set of statements that allows you to do the following:

- Execute a set of statements only if certain condition are met.
- Execute a set of statements zero or more times.
- Skip a set of statements.

We saw lots of examples of how switch can help us achieve our goals. Specifically the switch statement in Swift has become very powerful. It can match strings, range of values, have clauses in cases, or wildcard matches.

Chapter 8

Functions

Functions are self-contained blocks of code that perform a specific task. Swift's functions are very flexible. They can be very simple, such as the `print` function, or very complex. Here are some examples:

- They can be simple C-style functions with no parameter names.
- They can have local and external parameter names for parameters, similar to Objective-C.
- They can have parameters that provide default values.
- They can return multiple values.
- They can be passed as arguments.
- They can be returned as a result from other functions.
- They can have nested functions.

Defining Functions

The general format for a function starts with the keyword `func`, followed by the name of the function, optional arguments, and an optional return value.

```
func functionName([Parameters]) [-> returnValue] {
}
```

Items within the brackets [] are optional. Let's define a simple function called `greeting`:

```
func greeting(name : String) -> String {
    let greetingMessage = "Hello " + name
    return greetingMessage
}
```

This function takes one argument of type `String` and has a return value of type `String`. The body of the function prepends the word Hello to a name.

Calling a Function

To execute the code that the function represents is called "calling" a function. To call a function, you simply use the name of the function and any arguments that are required.

```
greeting("Waqar")
```

This calls the example function with an argument. Since we didn't capture the return value from the function, it's simply discarded. You can assign the result of the execution to a variable:

```
let mygreeting = greeting("Waqar")
```

You can also specify multiple arguments by separating each argument with a comma:

```
func greeting2(name1: String, name2 : String) -> String {
    let greetingMessage = "Hello " + name1 + " and " + name2
    return greetingMessage
}
let greeting2Message = greeting2("Waqar", name2: "Adam")
```

You can also have a function without any parameters:

```
func greeting0() -> String
{
    return "Hello, Swift"
}
let greeting0Message = greeting0()
```

Sometimes you want functions that don't return values. You don't need to specify the return type. In that case, the default is a return value `Void`.

```
func greeting3(name: String) {
    print("Hello " + name)
}
greeting("Waqar")
```

The return value is of type `Void`. If you wanted to be pedantic, you could write a function that actually returns a value of `Void`. The following code is equivalent to the preceding code:

```
func greeting3(name: String) -> Void {
    print("Hello " + name)
}
```

> **Note** Void is just an empty tuple, with no elements, that's written as ().

A function that's defined to have a return value must always return a value of a given type. If you'd like to return a nil, the return type must be defined as an optional.

```
func greeting3(name : String?) -> String? {
    if let theName = name {
        return "Hello " + theName
    }

    return nil
}
```

Functions can return multiple values. To do this, you must use the tuple type to box multiple values and return them:

```
func greeting4(name1 : String, name2 : String) -> (String, String) {
    let greeting1 = "Hello " + name1
    let greeting2 = "Hello " + name2

    return (greeting1, greeting2)
}
var greetings : (greeting1 : String, greeting2 : String) = greeting4("Waqar", name2:
"Mishal")

print(greetings.greeting1)
print(greetings.greeting2)
```

Parameter Names

All the functions we have defined have parameters names, such as name1 and name2. These names are available within the body of the function. The name of the first argument is not available outside the function body.

The functions that defined my caller function are unaware of the parameters. However, it can be useful for the caller function to know the purpose of the arguments. To solve this issue, Swift allows external parameter names that you can give to each parameter along with the local parameters. If you do not specify the external parameters, Swift will expose the internal argument variable names as the external variable names. The only exception is that the internal name for the first argument is not exposed by default. You can force it to have an external name for the first argument by adding an external name explicitly.

You specify the external parameter name before the local parameter name. Once you've defined the external parameter name, that name must be used when calling the function.

```
func greeting5(firstPersonName name1: String, secondPersonName name2 : String) -> String {
    let greetingMessage = "Hello " + name1 + " and " + name2

    return greetingMessage
}

let greeeting5Message = greeting5(firstPersonName: "Waqar", secondPersonName: "Mishal")
```

In this case, the local name and the external name are different. It's generally a better idea to use the external name as the internal name because that describes the parameter better. Doing that, the function looks like this:

```
func greeting2(firstPersonName: String, secondPersonName : String) -> String {
    let greetingMessage = "Hello " + firstPersonName + " and " + secondPersonName

    return greetingMessage
}
```

But this doesn't provide an external name for the first argument. Let's add that:

```
func greeting2(firstPersonName firstPersonName: String, secondPersonName: String) -> String {
    let greetingMessage = "Hello " + firstPersonName + " and " + secondPersonName

    return greetingMessage
}
```

If you want to omit the external names for the second and subsequent arguments, simply provide _ as the external name, but then it makes the code less readable.

```
func greeting6(firstname : String,  lastname : String) {
    print("Hello " + firstname + " " + lastname)
}

greeting6("Waqar","Malik")
```

Default Values

You can define default values for parameters when defining your function. If the default value for a parameter is defined, you can omit the parameter completely when calling if you would like to use the default value.

```
func greeting(name : String = "World") -> String {
    let greetingMessage = "Hello " + name
    return greetingMessage
}

let mygreeting = greeting()
let mygreeting = greeting( "Mishal")
```

The first call will use the default value for the name, and the second one will pass the value as an argument.

> **Note** Arrange the parameter list in such a way that the parameters with default values are at the end, so that the order of parameters looks the same for nondefault values when omitting default parameters.

Variadic Parameters

Sometimes you need a function that can take an unknown number of arguments. You can use three periods ... to specify a variadic parameter, which can take zero or more values. The arguments are made available inside the function as an array of the specific type.

```
func sum(numbers : Double...) -> Double {
    return numbers.reduce(0) {$0 + $1}
}

let mysum = sum(3.0, 5.0, 6.0)
```

> **Note** Functions can have only one variadic parameter, and it must always come at the very end of the parameter list. If the function has parameters with default values, the variadic parameter must come after all the defaulted variables, at the very end of the list.

Mutablity of Parameters

By default, parameters are passed as constants, and you can't change their values within the body of the function. Sometimes it is nice to be able to reuse a variable instead of defining a new one. To do so, you simply prefix the parameter with the `var` keyword:

```
func greeting(var name : String = "Waqar") -> String {
    name = "Hello " + name
    return name
}
```

> **Note** The changes made to the variable within the body of the function are available only within the function. They don't persist outside the function.

In-Out Parameters

If you'd like a parameter's value to exist outside the function, it must be marked as such using the `inout` keyword. When passing the variable to an `inout` parameter, the variable must be prefixed with an ampersand (&).

```
func tripleit(inout value : Double) {
    value *= 3
}

var value = 2.0
tripleit(&value)
print(value) // 6.0
```

Some restrictions apply to inout parameters. These parameters can't

- Have default values,
- Be variadic,
- Be passed as a constant,
- Be passed as a literal, or
- Be marked as var or let.

Function Types

When you define a function, its type is also created; the function types are made up of the arguments and return types.

```
func add(x: Double, y : Double) -> Double {
    return x + y
}
func multiply(x : Double, y : Double) -> Double {
    return x * y
}
```

These two functions have the same type; they have two arguments of type Double and return an argument of type Double. You write the function type as (Double, Double) -> Double. If you have a function that has no arguments and doesn't return a value, the type for that function is () -> ().

```
func myFunc () {
// Some computation
}
```

Now that you know that functions have a type, you can define a variable that can hold functions. We can use the type of the two math functions we defined earlier and define a variable. Then we can use that variable as a function.

```
var mathFunction : (Double, Double) -> Double
mathFunction = add
var result = mathFunction(3, 4) // 7

mathFunction = multiply
result = mathFunction(3, 4) // 12
```

Functions as Parameters

Since the variable is defined to take a specific type, you can make a new function that has the same type and assign it to this variable. You can also pass the function as an an argument to another function.

You define the function parameters as you'd define any other parameter:

```
func compute(computeFunction computeFunction: (Double, Double) -> Double, x : Double, y :
Double) -> Double {
    return computeFunction(x, y)
}

var result = compute(computeFunction: multiply, x: 3, y: 4)
```

In this function, we define the first argument as the function needed to compute the result; the other two are the values the function will take.

Functions as Return Values

You can take this one step further and have functions return other functions. Just define the return value for the function as a function type:

```
func computeFunction(type type : String) -> ((Double, Double) -> Double) {
    if(type == "+")
    {
        return add
    } else if type == "*" {
        return multiply
    } else {
        func myRand(x: Double, y : Double ) -> Double {
            return 42.0
        }
        return myRand
    }
}

mathFunction = computeFunction(type: "+")
result = mathFunction(3, 5)
```

Nested Functions

Most of the functions we have defined are global in scope, meaning they are available to everything in the module to use. In the previous example we defined a function named `myRand` within a function. That function is only available to be called within the function `computeFunction`. By combining all the preceding functions into one function, we have:

```
func computeFunction2(type type : String) -> ((Double, Double) -> Double) {
    func localAdd(x: Double, y : Double) -> Double {
        return x + y
    }

    func localMultiply(x : Double, y : Double) -> Double {
        return x * y
    }
```

```
    func myRand(x: Double, y : Double ) -> Double {
        return 42.0
    }

    if(type == "+")
    {
        return localAdd
    } else if type == "*" {
        return localMultiply
    } else {
        return myRand
    }
}
```

Summary

A function is a set of instructions that performs a specific task. It's a way to generalize functionality because it can be called multiple times or from different locations. In object-oriented programming, functions that belong to a specific object are called methods, but in Swift, methods are also declared using the `func` keyword.

Chapter 9

Closures

Closures are blocks of code that perform specific tasks; they can be passed around in your code. Closures in Swift are similar to blocks in C and Objective-C and to lambdas in some languages. Closures can capture and store references to constants and variables in the context in which they are defined. This is called "closing over" these constants and variables. Swift handles all the memory management required for capturing the environment.

The definition for closures is similar to that for functions, because in Swift functions are a special case of closures, with some differences:

- Global functions are closures that have a name and don't capture any values.
- Nested functions are closures that have a name but only capture values from the enclosing function.

Swift closure syntax is very clean with

- Inferred types for parameters and return types
- Implicit return from a single statement
- Shorthand argument names
- Trailing closure syntax

Closure Syntax

Closure syntax can get confusing depending how you define closure and how you use the closure To define a variable as a closure it is the same as defining another variable you have to choose if the closure variable is going to be a constant (`let`) or assignable (`var`), after that you have the name of the variable and then the actual type of the closure. The tricky part is how to define the type for closure. Closure type is similar to defining a function with arguments and return type:

```
var nameOfClosure : (arguments) -> (ReturnType)
var myClosure : (arg1 : Int) -> (Int)
```

You can also make the closure type optional just by including it in parentheses and adding the question mark.

```
var myClosure : ((arg1 : Int) -> (Int))?
```

Wouldn't it be nice instead of typing all those arguments and return types all the time? Yes, you can make an alias for the closure type by giving it a name, using the typealias keyword:

```
typealias MyClosureType = (arg1 : Int) -> (Int)
```

Now you can type MyClosureType instead of explicitly typing the whole arguments and return types.

```
var myClosure : MyClosureType
var myClosure : MyClosureType?
```

As with any other constant variable in Swift, you have to assess a value at the definition time, and you do the same with defining a constant closure type variable.

```
let myClosure = { ( parameters ) -> returnType in
        statements
}
```

Parameters can be of type:

- Constant
- Variable
- Inout
- Variadic (only if it's the last parameter)
- Tuple

Let's take a look at the global function called `sorted` in the standard Swift library. The function takes two arguments:

- An array with known types for elements.
- A closure that takes two arguments of the same type as the array elements and returns a Boolean. If the result is true, the first value will be stored before the second value in the new array. If the result is false, the second value will be stored before the first value.

The simplest and best-known way to handle this is to create a function that has the same signature as the closure and pass that as an argument. If you've used any of the sorting functions built into the C library, such as qsort, you know those functions have as their last argument a comparator function.

```
let numbers : [Int] = [119, 11, 45, 9, 34, 202]
func asending(element1 : Int, element2 : Int) -> Bool {
    return element1 < element2
}

let sortedNumbers1 = numbers.sort(asending)
```

The problem with this is you have to define each function ahead of time. Let's try this with a closure.

```
let sortedNumbers = numbers.sort{ (element1: Int, element2: Int) -> Bool in
    return element1 < element2
}
```

The inline closure looks almost identical to the function. We just removed the name, moved the arguments within the curly braces, and added the in keyword to denote the start of the closure block.

Inferring Types from Context

Since I defined the closure inline with the sorted functionn, the compiler can infer the types of the argument and the closure, so we don't have to specify them. Because we don't need to specify the types, I can also omit the parentheses and -> from the arguments and just specify the names of the arguments. The code is now even simpler:

```
sortedNumbers = numbers.sort( { element1, element2  in
    return element1 < element2
})
```

Implicit Returns

If the closure has one statement in the body and that one statement computes the return value of the closure, the closure can implicitly return that value and you can omit the return keyword.

```
sortedNumbers = numbers.sort({element1, element2 in element1 < element2})
```

Shorthand Argument Names

The arguments in an inline closure are automatically given internal names $0, $1, and so on, depending on the number of arguments. You can use those instead of the names you define. If you decide to use these names, you can omit the argument list and the in keyword as the inference system will correctly determine them. Then, the closure is made up solely of its body.

```
sortedNumbers = numbers.sort({ $0 < $1 })
```

Trailing Closures

If the function takes a closure as the final argument, you can move the closure expression outside of and after the parentheses. That's why it's recommended that you use trailing closures when defining functions.

```
sortedNumbers = numbes.sort() { $0 < $1 }
```

Capturing Values

We mentioned earlier that closures will capture variables and constants within the scope in which they are defined. The simplest examples of this are nested functions:

```
func capturingValues() {
    var a : Double = 5
    print(a)
    func increment(incrementBy : Double) {
        a += incrementBy
    }

    increment(4)
    print(a)

    increment(2)
    print(a)
}
```

Notice that we don't pass variable a into the body of the function, but the function still has access to the variable. We defined the function after defining the variable. In this case, the variable was captured because it was in the scope of the function when it was defined. If we define any variables after the function is defined, they won't be captured because they are not in the function's scope when the function was defined.

```
func capturingValues() {
    func increment(incrementBy : Double) {
        a += incrementBy
    }
    let a : Double = 5
    print(a)

    increment(4)
    print(a)

    increment(2)
    print(a)
}
```

This code would cause the Swift compiler to give an error because the variable was not in scope when the function was defined.

Since the closures capture variables strongly, this can lead to a memory issue called a retain cycle, which will be discussed in Chapter 15 (Memory Management and ARC). To solve this problem, you can explicitly state how to capture those variables. You specify the list of captured variables and how you would like to capture them before the arguments in the closure, if any.

```
{ [My Variable Capture List] (arugments) -> ReturnType in
}
```

This is helpful when accessing instance variables/functions of the class where this closure is defined. If you do not specify how to capture `self` and you reference a variable such as `self.myVariable`, or `self.myFunction()`, you will end up capturing `self` as a strong reference, which could cause a memory leak. To resolve this, you can specify to capture `self` with either the `weak` or `unowned` keyword, which will cause the compiler to make another pointer to `self` and pass it to the closure.

```
{[weak self] ...}

{[weak self] in
 if let strongSelf = self {
  strongSelf.dosomething()
}
}

{[weak self] in
 self?.dosomething()
}
```

this case self is captured as weak and therefore all of the optional syntax must be observed. The other is similar to forced unboxed syntax

```
{[unowned self] ... }
{[unowned self] in
        self.dosomething()
}
```

If you are not using self or any instance variables you don't need to do that.

Summary

You might already be familiar with the concept of closures. In Objective-C, they are called blocks. In Swift, blocks are imported as closures so you can use the two interchangeably. In Swift, functions are just named closures. You have to pay close attention to how closures capture the state of a program and how they can lead to memory cycles. You should be mindful when you use instance variables within closures.

Chapter 10

Enumerations

Enumeration is another type where you can group items of related values and use them in a type safe way in your code. In C/Objective-C you only had enumerations of type integer. But in Swift, enumerations have gotten quite an overhaul. You can define enumeration of type `String`, `Character`, `Int`, or a `floating` type; these also include variants of the types such as `Double`, `UInt`, etc.

Enumerations in Swift are first-class citizens, similar to Classes and Structures. They can do the following:

- Implement computed properties
- Instance methods
- Custom initializers to provide initial values
- Be extended
- Conform to protocols

Syntax

The basic syntax is the keyword `enum` and is then followed by the name of the enumeration. Notice the following three examples:

```
enum MyEnumeration {
// your case items
}
```

or

```
enum Suit {
    case Hearts
    case Spades
    case Diamonds
    case Clubs
}
```

or

```
enum Suit {
   case Hearts, Spades, Diamonds, Clubs
}
```

When we defined the above enumeration we did not define the type and did not implicitly give values. By default, these are defined as String types, and the initial values are the actual strings that make up the name for Clubs; it is initialized with "Clubs."

```
print(Suit.Clubs) // "Clubs\n"
```

But you cannot compare the values to actual strings because these enums are values themselves and can only be compared among each other.

```
if Suit.Hearts == "Hearts" { // Error

}
```

To initialized simply by creating variable either by explicitly giving a type of the enum or the one of the values for infer type.

```
let spades = Suit.Spades
let hearts : Suit = .Hearts
```

Once the type type of the value is assigned then we don't need to specify the type of the enum, just one of the values.

```
var suit = Suit.Clubs
suit = .Diamonds
```

Switch Statement and Enumerations

You can match individual values of the enumeration within the switch statement.

```
switch suit {
case .Hearts:
   print("Got Hearts")
case .Diamonds:
   print("Got Diamonds")
case .Spades:
   print("Got Spades")
}
```

As we discussed in Chapter 7 (Flow Control), for safety reasons the switch statement must be exhaustive. You can see that we left out the in the Clubs case; hence our code does not compile. We can also give a default case to match the rest of them.

```
switch suit {
case .Diamonds:
    print("Bling, Bling")
default:
    print("Not Bling")
}
```

Associated Values

Sometimes it is necessary to have a value along with the type: for instance we wanted the King or 10 of diamonds. To do that we define the enumeration case requiring type of values.

```
enum Suit2 {
    case Hearts(Int)
    case Spades(Int)
    case Diamonds(Int)
    case Clubs(Int)
}
```

Now we can define each individual card by requiring a value be passed when creating it. The value we will match in the case statement using the `let` syntax for each case. We will initialize each case item with an intial value.

```
let tenOfDiamonds = Suit2.Diamonds(10)
let aceOfDiamonds = Suit2.Diamonds(1)
```

You can still do this:

```
switch tenOfDiamonds {
case .Diamonds:
    print("Bling")
default:
    print("Not Bling")
}
```

How do you extract the associated values or use the let or var keyword and a variable name in the match case?

```
switch aceOfDiamonds {
case .Diamonds(let value):
    print("\(value)")
default:
    break;
}
```

In our case we only associated one value for each case and same type (Int). You can associate more than one value and different types to each case.

```
enum MyEnum {
    case One(Int)
    case Two(String)
    case Three(Int, Int)
    case Four(Int, String)
    case Five(Int, Int, Float, Character, String)
}
```

Each of these cases has a different number and types of values associated with them, to initialize

```
let five = MyEnum.Five(1, 4, 9.3, "C", "Test")
switch five {
case .Three(let first, let second):
    print("\(first + second)")
case .Five(let first, let second, var third, let forth, let fifth):
    print("\(first) \(second) \(third) \(forth) \(fifth)")
default:
    break;
}
```

You can also move the let or var outside before the match if you wanted to extract all values:

```
switch five {
case .Three(let first, let second):
    print("\(first + second)")
case let .Five(first, second, third, forth, fifth):
    print("\(first) \(second) \(third) \(forth) \(fifth)")
default:
    break;
}
```

But in this case all the value will be let or var; you cannot be intermixed.

Raw Values

In the previous section we associated some values to each case type. An alternative to associated value is the raw values; each case can come with predefined values associated with them, but they have to be of the same type. Let's redefine our cards Suit using the Character type and assign some default values.

```
enum Suit : Character {
    case Hearts = "♥"
    case Spades = "♠"
    case Diamonds = "♦"
    case Clubs = "♣"
}
```

The raw values are limited to Strings, Characters, Ints, and Floats (or variations such as `Int8` or `UInt16`), and each value must be unique for each case.

> **Note** The raw values are not like associated values; they are constant for each time and they are defined at compile time instead of runtime.

Since we defined our `Suit` as `Character` type, explicit value must be assigned to each case. If you define your enum using integers or strings as raw values you do not need to explicitly assign each values; they can be inferred.

```
enum Suit : Int {
    case Hearts
    case Spades
    case Diamonds
    case Clubs
}
```

By default enums with raw values of integer types start with 0(zero) implicitly. If you wanted to start with a different value or assign different values to each case you could do that as well.

```
enum Suit : Int {
    case Hearts = 5
    case Spades
    case Diamonds
    case Clubs
}
```

In this example the `Hearts` is assigned the value 5 and then `Spades` will get the next integer 6 and so forth.

```
enum Suit : Int {
    case Hearts = 15
    case Spades = 1
    case Diamonds = 16
    case Clubs = 38
}
```

Now let's define Suit based on the String type. We did not explicitly assign values to each case; they were inferred by the characters that make up the case.

```
enum Suit : String {
    case Hearts
    case Spades
    case Diamonds
    case Clubs
}
```

or you can explicitly assign values to them

```
enum Suit : String {
    case Hearts = "Herz"
    case Spades = "Laub"
    case Diamonds = "Schellen"
    case Clubs = "Eichel"
}
```

Now that we have defined the enum using the raw values, how do we access those values? Enum type defines a property called rawValue, which can be used to access those values

```
let heart = Suit.Hearts.rawValue
print(heart)
print(Suit.Hearts.rawValue)
```

You can create an enumeration type using the raw value using the init(rawValue:) method; this is a failable initializer: it will either return an enumeration type or nil; the enumeration type will be an optional type that you will have to unbox before it can be matched.

```
let theSpades = Suit(rawValue: "Hearts") // valid raw value
let possibleSuit = Suit(rawValue: "TheHearts") // invalid raw value
```

Recursive Enumerations

Let's say you go to your favorite pizza place and order a pizza; they have predefined pizza types:

```
enum PizzaType {
    case Mushrooms
    case Olives
    case Pepperoni
}
```

That is good if you wanted to order the whole pizza of one topping, but most of us like to mix different type of toppings (i.e., we are mixing two types of pizzas). Let's add a case that takes two different toppings. We could do this by adding a few more cases now that our case items are getting out of hand, Most pizza places have 10 or more toppings listed and picking 3 out of 10, the combinations get pretty long.

```
enum PizzaType {
    case Mushrooms
    case Olives
    case Pepperoni
    case MushroomsOlives
    case MushroomsPeppроni
    case OlivesPepperoni
    case MushroomsOlivesPepperoni
}
```

It would be really nice if we could have cases where you are allowed to mix different pizza types, something like this:

```
enum PizzaType {
    case Mushrooms
    case Olives
    case Pepperoni
    case Custom2(PizzaType, PizzaType)
    case Custom3(PizzaType, PizzaType, PizzaType)
}
```

But if that was the case then you would be adding yourself recursively and would keep adding *ad infinitum. This would cause your compiler to go insane. That is why this is not allowed.*

To fix this problem Swift provides you with an indirect keyword. You can either define the who enum as indirect or specific cases.

```
enum PizzaType {
    case Mushrooms
    case Olives
    case Pepperoni
    indirect case Custom2(PizzaType, PizzaType)
    indirect case Custom3(PizzaType, PizzaType, PizzaType)
}

let myPizza = PizzaType.Custom2(.Olives, .Mushrooms)

indirect enum PizzaType {
    case Mushrooms
    case Olives
    case Pepperoni
    case Custom2(PizzaType, PizzaType)
    case Custom3(PizzaType, PizzaType, PizzaType)
}
```

Now if you add any other simple topping such as capers, our custom pizzas can be created with combination of new toppings without having to explicitly add the combinations of toppings.

Summary

As you can see from all the examples, enumerations are much more than simple collections of similar types. They are very powerful and allow you to write type safe programs

Specifically the recursive nature of the enumeration type can give you almost infinite combinations without having to define each explicitly.

Chapter 11

Classes and Structures

Unlike in other languages, in Swift, classes and structures are very similar, with only few features that separate them. So as we describe and discuss the functionality of objects, this applies to both classes and structures. We will point out where they differ.

Commonality

Here are some of the things that the classes and structures have in common:

- Properties to store values
- Methods to provide functionality
- Initializers
- Extensibility
- Conformance to protocols

Classes have some additional properties and capabilities that structures lack:

- Inheritance; classes can have parent classes, structures can't.
- Deinitializers; classes have them, structures don't.
- Reference counting; classes use reference counting to manage memory.
- Runtime support for type casting.
- Classes are passed by reference while structures are copied when passed around.

Some languages use two files for classes: one for the interface and one for the implementation. Like Java, Swift uses only one file, with a `.swift` extension. You generally create one file per class or structure and give it the same name as the class. If we were creating a `Person` class, we would name the file `Person.swift`.

> **Note** Unlike Objective-C, Swift classes don't require a parent class. And use single inheritance for class hierarchy.

Definition

You use either the `class` or `struct` keywords, depending on whether you're creating a class or structure. Here's the syntax:

```
class [name of class] {
        // class definition
}

struct [name of struct] {
        // struct definition
}
```

When you define a `struct` or `class` in Swift, you're creating a new data type. Swift follows the `UpperCamelCase` format for names for types; they start with an uppercase letter and each successive word also starts with an uppercase letter, for example, `MyType`, `SomeFancyType`. This is a convention but not a requirement. Now let's look at a `struct`:

```
struct Point {
    var x = 0.0
    var y = 0.0
}
```

We define a structure called `Point` that has two properties called x and y. We defined x and y as variables, but you can also have constants using the `let` keyword. We initialized the values to some good default values. The types are inferred to be `double` by the compiler. Let's keep going:

```
class Engine {
    var numberOfCylinders : Int = 4
}
```

Here's a class named Engine. For now, its only property is the number of cylinders. We gave it a default value of 4.

We have only defined the two new types; they have to be instantiated before we can use them. The syntax for creating an instance of either a `class` or a `struct` is the same:

```
var location = Point()
var smallEngine = Engine()
```

When you instantiate a type, there is an initializer function that is called init; this is a special name .If the do no override the default initializer `init()` then the compiler will create a default one for you.

Initialization

Initialization is a process in preparing the class to a known state that can be used safely. This includes setting all stored properties to a known valid value, and another setup is needed before the developer can use the instance of that type. The process of initialization is handled by the `init` functions of the given type. Let's rewrite our engine class to have an initializer:

```
class Engine1 {
    var numberOfCylinders: Int
    init () {
        numberOfCylinders = 4
    }
}
```

This does not help us much, since it always creates an engine with 4 cylinders. What if we wanted to create an engine with 6 cylinders? We could create an engine with 4 cylinders and then change the value of the property to 6; it works but exposes the inner workings of the class. A better way would be to pass the value of the number of cylinders needed.

```
class Engine1 {
    var numberOfCylinders: Int
    init () {
        numberOfCylinders = 4
    }

    init (numberOfCylinders : Int) {
        self.numberOfCylinders = numberOfCylinders
    }
}
```

Now that is better, we now have two initializers. But suppose we have to do some other setup, either based on number of cylinders or in general? There are few ways to solve this issue:

- Duplicate the additional code in the initializer
- Create a new private function that we can call from each of those initializers
- Remove the initializer without arguments and just use one with the argument.

Each of these options have their drawbacks, but we can address those drawbacks by adding default values to the arugment of the initializer function. This way, we can combine both the initializer functions into one and get the same functionality.

```
class Engine1 {
    var numberOfCylinders: Int
    init (numberOfCylinders : Int = 4) {
        self.numberOfCylinders = numberOfCylinders
    }
}
```

That is good, but we have not done any error checking on the input value. What if the user creates an engine with 0 cylinders, which we could still accept as it could be an electric car, but we are making fossil fuel-based engines for now. How about negative cylinders? What kind of engine that would be! For today's technology we will limit the number of cylinders to between 1 and 12. Swift provides a way to not create an instance of type if the inputs are invalid; it is called an optional initializer. The optional initializer is declared the same way, but with the addition of ? to the name so `init?()`. One difference is that it can return a nil when not creating and initializing the type. That is why the type returned will always be an optional; if you try to assign the resulting value to a non optional variable, you will have to unbox it, either explicitly or using the `if-let` syntax.

```
class Engine1 {
    var numberOfCylinders: Int
    init?(numberOfCylinders : Int = 4) {
        guard numberOfCylinders > 1 && numberOfCylinders <= 12 else {
            self.numberOfCylinders = 4
            return nil
        }
        self.numberOfCylinders = numberOfCylinders
    }
}
```

Accessing Properties

Both of the objects we defined have some properties. To access them you can use the dot (.) syntax.

```
print(smallEngine.numberOfCylinders)
print(location.x)
```

> **Note** Access control restricts access to certain parts of the code, which allows you to hide implementation details of your types. We will discuss access control at length in another chapter. For now, we will use the default access control for types.

Here's how you assign new values to properties:

```
smallEngine.numberOfCylinders = 5
location.x = 10
location.y = 30
```

You can drill down into the properties and access them .

```
class Automobile {
    var engine = Engine();
    var numberOfWheels = 4
}
var car = Automobile()
car.engine.numberOfCylinders = 6
```

Value Types vs. Reference Types

A value type is one whose value is copied when it's assigned to a variable or when passed as a function parameter.

```
var anotherLocation = location
location.x = 20
location.y = 50

print(location.x) // 20
print(anotherLocation.x) // 10
```

When we assign the point value to `anotherLocation`, Swift creates a copy of the object and assigns the existing values from the `location` object. If we change the value of the original location, we won't affect the value of the new variable.

> **Note** All basic types in Swift are value types. They are implemented as structures.

Reference types are types whose values are not copied. Instead, a reference to an existing object is copied. Classes in Swift are reference types.

```
let myCar = car
car.engine.numberOfCylinders = 10
print(myCar.engine.numberOfCylinders)
```

This code creates another variable called `myCar`, which refers to the existing object. When we change the value of `numberOfCylinders` for the original car, we also change the values of the properties of `myCar`. Those properties point to the same location in memory that holds the original car.

But, you say, `myCar` is declared as a constant. How can you change the value of a constant? With reference types you define the variable that it points to, to be a constant. In this example, `myCar` can't point to any other car. If you try something like `myCar = Car()`, you'll get an error, because you're trying to point to another location.

> **Note** Reference types in Swift are similar to pointers in C/C++/Objective-C. They are better in Swift in that you don't have to use the dereference operator (*).

Now you know that classes in Swift are reference types, and that it's possible to have multiple variables point to the same object. How can you find out if two variables point to the same instance of the object? Swift provides two operators:

- Identical to (===)
- Not identical to (!==)

```
if myCar === car {
    print("Both myCar and car are the same instance of the Car")
}
```

The identity operator (===) is different from the equality operator (==). Suppose you and your friend go to the Apple store and purchase identical iPhones. The phones are equal (==) to each other because they have the same feature set, but they are not the same phone so the identity operator would fail.

Choosing Between Classes or Structures

Most of the time you'll want to create classes for your objects, but there are few situations where you should use structures instead.

- If you want to copy the object when passing it around.
- If the properties of the object themselves are value types.
- If the object doesn't inherit from other types.
- If you want to expose Swift type in Objective-C.

If you were building a tree data structure, you'd want the node to be a structure, and the tree itself to be a class.

What if you want your nested class to be used only within the enclosing class? Swift provides three levels of access control.

Properties

We already used properties in an example, but only one type of property so far. There are actually two types of properties:

- *Stored properties* store some values for an instance of your class.
- *Computed properties* compute the values.

> **Note** Enumerations can't use stored properties, only classes and structures can.

Stored Properties

In the `Engine` class example we have one stored property called `numberOfCylinders`. Stored properties can be either mutable using the `var` keyword or immutable using the `let` keyword. We can also provide a default value for the property. You can override these default values during the initialization of the class, even for `let` keyword properties.

```
class Engine {
    let numberOfCylinders : Int

    init(numberOfCylinders: Int) {
        self.numberOfCylinders = numberOfCylinders
    }
}
```

The property numberOfCylinders is set in the init; if you try to set the value outside the init method, Swift will give an error. If we were to set the default value for numberOfCylinders when declaring the variable, we will not be able to change that value in the init method.

> **Note** When using let values, do not set the default values when declaring the variable, otherwise you will not be able to set the value in the init method.

Lazy Stored Properties

Sometimes you need to wait to calculate the value of a stored property until the initialization has taken place. You mark such properties with the lazy keyword. These properties are useful when the functionality may never be used.

> **Note** Lazy properties must be of var type, as they might be initialized outside of the init methods.

```
class Automobile {
    lazy var engine = Engine(numberOfCylinders: 6)
    var numberOfWheels = 4
}
```

In the preceding code, we marked the engine property as lazy, even though we initialized it with the init method. The init method won't be executed until we access the engine property. Now look at the following:

```
class Engine {
    var numberOfCylinders : Int = 4
    init (numberOfCylinders : Int) {
        self.numberOfCylinders = numberOfCylinders
        print("Engine Init function Called \(self.numberOfCylinders)")
    }
}

class Automobile {
    var engine = Engine(numberOfCylinders: 4)
    var numberOfWheels : Int = 4
}
```

```
class Automobile2 {
    lazy var engine = Engine(numberOfCylinders : 6)
    var numberOfWheels : Int = 4
}

func create () {
    var car1 = Automobile()
    var car2 = Automobile2()
}

create() // Engine Init function Called 4
```

Because we don't access the car2 engine, it's never created.

Computed Properties

These properties don't store any values. Instead, they provide a getter and a setter to provide values based on other properties. The syntax for these properties is:

```
var propertyName : PropertyType {
  get {
    return someValue
  }
  set(value) {
  }
}

class Automobile {
    class Engine {
        var numberOfCylinders : Int = 0
        var started : Bool = false
        init(numberOfCylinders: Int) {
            self.numberOfCylinders = numberOfCylinders
        }
    }
    let engine : Engine
    let numberOfWheels : Int

    var started : Bool {
        get {
            return self.engine.started
        }
        set(started) {
            self.engine.started = started
        }
    }
    init (numberOfCylinders : Int, numberOfWheels : Int) {
        engine = Engine(numberOfCylinders: numberOfCylinders)
        self.numberOfWheels = numberOfWheels;
    }
}
```

```
var fastCar = Automobile(numberOfCylinders: 6, numberOfWheels: 4)
print("Car started \(fastCar.started)") // false
fastCar.started = true
print("Car started \(fastCar.started)") // true
```

You can skip the argument declaration for the setter. Swift will automatically create a variable called `newValue`, and you can access that within the setter.

```
set {
    self.engine.started = newValue
}
```

If you provide a getter but no setter, the computed property becomes a read-only property. Even though it's a read-only property, it's not a constant and can't be declared as such with the `let` keyword.

Property Observers

You can add property value change observers to any stored property. These observers are called whenever a new value is set, even if the value will remain the same. Observers are not called when a property is first initialized.

> **Note** You can't add property observers to `lazy` stored properties.

You can also add observers to inherited properties; they can be either stored or computed by overriding them in a subclass.

You can implement either or both of the following observers on a property:

- `willSet` is called before the value is changed.
- `didSet` is called after the value is changed.

The following code shows both:

```
class Engine {
        var numberOfCylinders : Int = 0 {
            willSet(cylinderCount) {
                print("about to set the cylinder count \(cylinderCount)")
            }
            didSet {
                print("engine now has \(self.numberOfCylinders) cylinders")
            }
        }
        var started : Bool = false
        init(numberOfCylinders: Int) {
            self.numberOfCylinders = numberOfCylinders
        }
    }
```

You can omit the new value argument in the willSet observer if you want. In that case, you can access the new value by using the variable name newValue.

The didSet observer doesn't provide an argument for the old value, but you can still access it using the oldValue variable within the observer:

```
class Engine {
    var numberOfCylinders : Int = 0 {
        willSet{
            print("about to set the cylinder count \(newValue)")
        }
        didSet {
            print("engine had \(oldValue) cylinders")
            print("engine now has \(self.numberOfCylinders) cylinders")
        }
    }
    var started : Bool = false
    init(numberOfCylinders: Int) {
        self.numberOfCylinders = numberOfCylinders
    }
}
```

Type Properties

All the properties we have used are instance properties because they belong to a specific instance of the object. If you create an engineA and an engineB, both will have their own properties called numberOfCylinders that aren't shared between the two. The syntax is:

```
struct MyStruct {
        static var storedTypeProperty = "Some Value"
        static val computedProperty : Int {
                return someInt
        }
}

enum MyEnum {
        static var storedTypeProperty = "Some Value"
        static var computedProperty : Int {
                return someInt
        }
}

class MyClass {
        class var computedProperty : Int {
                return someInt

        }
}
```

To access those properties, you use the dot syntax, and you use the object type instead of an instance of the type, like so:

```
print(MyStruct.storedTypeProperty)
MyStruct.storedTypeProperty = "New Value"
```

Summary

In object-oriented programming in Swift, custom objects or types are the basis of programs. In Swift, even basic types such as `Int` and `Double` are value types and are defined as structures, which allow you to extend basic types with your own convenience functions.

You learned the difference between value types and reference types and saw how to choose the best solution for your specific problem. You also learned what properties are and how to use them effectively.

Chapter 12

Methods

A subroutine is a block of code that performs a specific task. Another name for a subroutine is a function. You've already seen global functions, such as `print`. Methods are functions that are associated with a particular type. In Swift, methods can be associated with classes, structures, and enumeration types. There are two types of methods: instance methods and type methods.

Instance Methods

Instance methods are those that belong to a particular instance of a class. You have to create an object to use those methods. They are defined just like standalone functions, but within the class scope:

```
class Stack {
    private var stack = [Double]()

    func isEmpty () -> Bool {
        return self.stack.isEmpty
    }

    func peek () -> Double? {
        return self.stack.last
    }
        func pop () -> Double? {
        let value = self.stack.last
        if nil != value {
            self.stack.removeLast()
        }
        return value
    }

    func push (item : Double) {
        self.stack.append(item)
    }
}
```

The Stack class implements four instance methods and a property that stores the values for the stack.

To use the instance methods, you create an instance of the Stack and then use the dot notation to invoke methods:

```
var stack = Stack()
// crate a new instance of stack

println(stack.isEmpty())
// check if the stack is empty prints true

stack.push(5)
// push a value of 5 on top of the stack

println(stack.isEmpty())
// Check if the stack is empty prints false

var value = stack.peek()
// See what value is the top of the stack

stack.push(103)
// push another value

value = stack.pop()
// get the top value
```

The argument names for methods have the same rules as for functions.

To call an instance method within another method, you can use the dot notation and the self keyword. The use of self is optional—it's inferred. The only exception is when the parameter name is the same as the method name, in which case the parameter name takes precedence.

> **Note** Self is a special property that gets created for each instance of the type. It refers to that specific instance of the type and can only be used within that instance.

We can rewrite the class like this:

```
class Stack {
    private var stack = [Double]()

    func isEmpty () -> Bool {
        print("local Empty")
        return stack.count.isEmpty
    }
```

```
    func peek () -> Double? {
        return stack.last
    }

    func pop () -> Double? {
        let value = stack.last
        if nil != value {
            stack.removeLast()
        }
        return value
    }

    func push (item : Double) {
        stack.append(item)
    }
}
```

Modifying Type State

One of the differences between classes, as opposed to structures and enumeration types, is that in structs and enums methods by default don't allow modifying of the state or the values of properties.

```
struct SomeStruct {
    var value = 0.0
    func updateValueBy(someValue : Double ) {
        value = value + someValue
    }
}
```

In this example, the updateValueBy function is trying to update the property value but this is not allowed. You can opt-in to the mutating behavior of the method by prefixing the method with the mutating keyword.

```
struct SomeStruct {
    var value = 0.0
    mutating func updateValueBy(someValue : Double ) {
        value = value + someValue
    }
}
```

You can't call mutating methods for structures declared as constants. The following code would result in an error; because myStruct is defined using the let keyword, it's immutable.

```
let myStruct = SomeStruct()
myStruct.updateValueBy(10)
```

In structures, you can even assign a new value to `self` in mutating methods.

```
struct SomeStruct {
    var value = 0.0
    mutating func updateValueBy(someValue : Double ) {
        self = SomeStruct(value + someValue)
    }
}
```

The mutating methods of an enumeration type can set the `self` to a different member value of the type.

```
enum SomeEnum {
    case value1, value2
    mutating func toggle () {
        switch self {
        case value1:
            self = value2
        case value2:
            self = value1
        }
    }
}
var myEnum = SomeEnum.value1
myEnum.toggle()
```

Type Methods

Type methods are those that belong to a particular type. You don't need to create a specific instance of an object to use those. For classes, you use the keyword `class` before a method definition and for a `struct` you use the `static` keyword. And to call those methods, you use the type name instead of a particular instance of type.

```
class SomeClass {
    class func typeMethod() {

    }
}

SomeClass.typeMethod()

struct SomeStruct {
    static func staticFunc () {
    }
}

SomeStruct.staticFunc()
```

Summary

Methods are the basis for creating and extending types. They help you structure code in a reusable set of instructions. There are two types of methods: instance methods and type methods. Methods are the interface to the types; they help you hide the implementation details. You can override methods in subclasses or extend the existing type by adding methods. This allows you to make a type very versatile, so you can avoid writing duplicate code.

Chapter 13

Inheritance

When you write an object-oriented program, the classes and objects you create have relationships with one another. They work together to make your program do its thing.

Two aspects of OOP are most important when dealing with relationships between classes and objects. The first is **inheritance**, the subject of this chapter. When you create a new class, it's often useful to define the new class in terms of its differences from an already existing class. Using inheritance, you can define a class that has all the capabilities of a parent class: it *inherits* those capabilities. You can have a general class called `Automobile`, for example, that defines a vehicle for operation on roads, typically with four wheels, such as a truck or car. `Automobile` can define some basic properties that constitute an automobile, and then you can create a specialized automobile by defining a `Car` type that will inherit from `Automobile`. It will get its properties from `Automobile` so you don't have to redefine them. You only add new properties that make it a Car type. This is inheritance because `Car` inherits the `Automobile`'s properties.

The other OOP technique used with related classes is **composition**, in which objects contain references to other objects. For example, a Car type in a racing simulator might have four tire objects it uses during game play. When your object keeps references to others, you can take advantage of features offered by the others; that's composition.

Terminology

- **Superclass** or **parent class** is the class you are inheriting from.
- **Subclass** or **child class** is the class that is inheriting.
- **Override** is when you replace the implementation of a method in the parent class with a method in the child class.
- Any class that does not inherit from a class is called a **base class**.

> **Note** Unlike Objective-C, Swift classes do not require a common parent base class such as NSObject.

Defining a Base Class

Let's define a base class called Shape that we'll use to extend and draw specific types of shapes:

```
class Shape {
    var fillColor : UIColor
    var bounds : CGRect

    init(bounds : CGRect, fillColor : UIColor) {
        self.bounds = bounds
        self.fillColor = fillColor
    }

    func draw () {
        print("I don't know how to draw this shape.")
    }
}
var shape = Shape(bounds: CGRectZero, fillColor: UIColor.redColor())
shape.draw()
```

This class has two properties, the fill color and the bounding box, and a method called `draw` to draw the desired shape. In the base class we don't draw any shape because we have to create a specialized class that knows how to draw the shape.

Subclassing

Swift only allows single inheritance, which means that a subclass can only have a single parent class. Some languages, notably C++, allow multiple inheritance in which a child class can have more than one parent class. Since protocols are also first class citizens in Swift you can inherit class from a protocol using the same syntax.

The syntax for Swift subclassing is simple: when defining a subclass you add a colon and then the name of the parent class.

```
class Subclass : Superclass {
}
```

Let's extend the Shape class and specialize it to draw a circle

```
class Circle: Shape {
}

shape = Circle(bounds: CGRectMake(0.0, 0.0, 30.0, 30.0), fillColor: UIColor.blueColor())
shape.draw()
```

We defined a new class called `Circle` that has the `Shape` parent class. `Circle` inherits the `bounds` and `fillColor` properties of the parent class. It also inherits the `draw` method and the initializer method as well. We will use the `init` method from the parent class because we don't need to change it. But we are going to override the `draw` method to draw the circle.

Any method that's `internal` or public permissions can be overridden; you just need to add `override` before the definition of the method.

```
class Circle: Shape {
    override func draw() {
        print("Drawing a circle in a bounding box \(NSStringFromCGRect(self.bounds)) and
color \(self.fillColor.description)")
    }
}
```

The following items can be overridden in Swift

- Instance methods
- Type methods
- Instance properties
- Type properties
- Subscripts

Let's create another subclass of the `Shape` class and call it `Polygon`. (We will assume it is regular polygon, such as equilateral triangle or square)

```
class Polygon : Shape {
    var numberOfSides : Int = 3
    override func draw() {
        print("Drawing a polygon with \(numberOfSides) sides in a bounding box
        \(NSStringFromCGRect(self.bounds)) and color \(self.fillColor.description)")
    }
}

shape = Polygon(bounds: CGRectMake(0.0, 0.0, 30.0, 30.0), fillColor: UIColor.blueColor())
shape.draw()
```

If you want to access the superclass's methods from the subclass, you replace the reference to self with super. Let's say a user sets the number of sides to an invalid value and the program doesn't know how to draw the polygon. You could ask the parent to draw the shape, but in this case the parent doesn't know how to draw so it simply prints that message. You can also use super with any other method.

```
class Polygon : Shape {
    var numberOfSides : Int = 3
    override func draw() {
        if numberOfSides <= 0 {
            super.draw()
        } else {
            print("Drawing a polygon with \(numberOfSides) sides in a bounding box
\(NSStringFromCGRect(self.bounds)) and color \(self.fillColor.description)")
        }
    }
}
```

Properties

You can override the getters and setters for inherited properties or add custom observers. The overriding of the getters and setters works with both stored and computed properties. The subclass doesn't know if the inherited property is stored or computed. To override, you have to specify both the name and the type of the property.

For inherited properties that are read-only in the superclass, you can provide both setter and getter to make the property read-write. If a property is read-write in the super class, you can't make is read-only in the subclass.

You can't add property observers to inherited constant stored properties or inherited read-only computed properties for obvious reasons. You can't provide both an overriding setter and an overriding property observer for the same property. Simply observe it in the setter. The following example shows how to override properties to observe and to provide a custom setter and getter.

```
class Circle: Shape {
    override var fillColor : UIColor {
        didSet {
            println("the new color is \(self.fillColor)")
        }
    }

    override var bounds : CGRect {
        get {
            return super.bounds
        }
        set (newBounds) {
            super.bounds = CGRectInset(newBounds, 5, 5)
        }
    }
```

```
    override func draw() {
        print("Drawing a circle in a bounding box \(NSStringFromCGRect(self.bounds)) and
color \(self.fillColor.description)")
    }
}
```

Preventing Overriding

All this freedom is good, but sometimes you want to prevent those using your code from overriding some parts. You can do that by marking your methods, properties, classes, and subscripts as final:

- `final func`
- `final class func`
- `final var`
- `final subscript`

You can even mark a whole class as final to prevent users from subclassing.

```
final class Myclass {
}
```

Any attempt to override or subclass items marked with the final keyword will result in an error.

Summary

You learned a key concept in object-oriented programming called inheritance. Inheritance provides a powerful way to design and modularize programs. When you start to develop your programs, you will be extending classes and methods to customize them for your needs.

Chapter 14

Extensions

When you write object-oriented programs, you'll often want to add some new behavior to an existing class. For example, you might have designed a new kind of tire, so you'd subclass Tire and add the new, cool stuff. When you want to add behavior to an existing class, you often create a subclass.

But sometimes subclassing isn't convenient. For example, to add some new behavior to `String`, you can sublass the string as your own string type such as `MyString`, but what if you're using a toolkit or library they will have no knowledge of this new new class. When the toolkit or library return a string it will be returned as the original string type, you will end up converting those `String` type to `MyString` every time if you wanted to use new functionality in your string class.

The dynamic runtime dispatch mechanism employed by Swift lets you add methods to existing classes. The Swift term for these new methods is **extensions**.

You can add extensions to classes, structures, protocol, and enums. Since basic types such as Int are structs, you can even extend them and add functionality.

> **Note** Extensions are analogous to categories in Objective-C. However, in Objective-C, each category must have a name, while extensions in Swift do not have names.

With extensions you can add:

- computed properties
- static computed properties
- instance and type methods
- initializers
- define subscripts
- define and use new nested types
- make an existing type conform to a protocol

> **Note** Extensions can't override existing functionality; they can only add new functionality. Extensions cannot have stored properties.

You can even extend protocols so any other type conforming the protocol will get that extended functionaly.

Creating an Extension

The syntax for adding an extension to an existing type is:

```
extension ExistingType {
    // your additions
}
```

To extend an existing type to conform to one or more protocols, simply specify the protocols as you'd define a class or structure:

```
extension ExistingType : Protocol1, Protocol2 {
   // protocol additions
}
```

If you look that the Apple definition for Array structure, they have added an extension to the base Array structure, and one of the function they have added is removeLast

```
/// Remove an element from the end of the Array in O(1).
/// Requires: count > 0
mutating func removeLast() -> Element
```

Apple has not defined a function that removes the first element. Let's add that convenience method:

```
extension Array {
    mutating func removeFirst() -> Element {
        let firstObject = self.removeAtIndex(0)
        return firstObject
    }
}
```

Since we added this method, it will be available to all instances of Array types even if they were created before we added this method.

Computed Properties

Extensions can add computed instance and type properties to existing types. Look at the class Circle from Chapter 13. If I want to extend Circle to return the area of the circle or the circumference, we can add couple of computed properties. Since we defined this class, we could just add these as a normal method. If we didn't have access to the implementation or wanted to separate the implementation, we would use an extension.

```
let π = 3.141
extension Circle {
    var radius : Double {
        let width = Double(self.bounds.size.width)
        return width / 2.0
    }

    var area : Double {
        let radius = self.radius
        return (π * radius * radius)
    }
}
```

We defined two properties—the first one computes the radius of the circle and the second one then computes the area of the circle.

Since these are read-only properties, We don't need to define the set methods. Extensions can't add stored properties or add observers to existing properties.

Initializers

Extensions can add new initializers to existing types. This gives you the power to initialize types with your custom types that the system doesn't know about.

> **Note** Extensions can't add designated initializers or deinitializers to the class.

Let' say you defined a type that you need to initialize as an existing type. You could just initialize the existing type and then assign different values, but you'd have to do that every time you create a new type. Or you could just define an initializer that encapsulates that logic.

```
extension UIColor {
    convenience init(rgba : UInt32) {
        let r = CGFloat(Double(rgba >> 24 & 0xFF) / 255.0)
        let g = CGFloat(Double(rgba >> 16 & 0xFF) / 255.0)
        let b = CGFloat(Double(rgba >> 8 & 0xFF) / 255.0)
        let a = CGFloat(Double(rgba & 0xFF) / 255.0)

        self.init(red: r, green: g, blue: b, alpha: a)
    }
}

let color = UIColor(rgba: 0xff0000ff)
```

In this example we define an extension to `UIColor` to take an unsigned integer and create a color instance.

> **Note** When you define an initializer in an extension, you are still responsible for making sure that each instance is fully initialized once the initializer completes.

Methods

You've already seen how to add methods. You can add both instance methods and type methods to an existing type.

Using the convenience `init` method we can extend the `UIColor` class some more by adding a type method.

```
extension UIColor {
      class func colorWithRGBAHex(rgba : UInt32) -> UIColor? {
                return UIColor(rgba: rgba)
          }
}
let color = UIColor.colorWithRGBAHex(0x00ff00ff)!
```

Mutating Methods

If the type you're adding with the extension is a structure or an enumeration type and you need to modify the state of the object, you must use the mutating keyword just as you would when adding methods when creating the original type.

You saw earlier that we added a method to an Array type. Because the Array type is defined as a struct in Swift and not as a class, we had to add the mutating keyword in front of the method.

In Swift, the basic Int type is a structure. We can even extend it by adding some methods:

```
extension Int {
    mutating func doubleIt() {
        self = 2 * self
    }
}

var myint = Int(5)
myint.doubleIt()
```

Subscripts

Extensions can add a subscript to existing types. You saw an example of a Stack type in chapter 10. Suppose you wanted to peek at the nth element from the top if it exists. You could do so with the following:

```
extension Stack {
    subscript(index : Int) -> Double? {
        if self.stack.count < index {
            return self.stack[index]
        }
        return nil
    }
}
var stack = Stack()
stack.push(5)
stack.push(103)
print(stack[1])
```

Nested Types

With extensions you can even add nested types to existing types (classes, structures, and enumerations). This example adds the error type enum to UIColor to return a color based on the error type. We added a new type called ErrorKind.

```
extension UIColor {
    enum ErrorKind : Int {
        case Normal, File, API
    }
```

```
    class func errorColor(errorKind : ErrorKind) -> UIColor? {
        var color : UIColor? = nil
        switch errorKind {
        case .Normal:
            color = colorWithRGBAHex(0xff0000ff)
        case .File :
            color = colorWithRGBAHex(0xcc0000ff)
        case .API:
            color = colorWithRGBAHex(0xaa0000ff)
        }

        return color
    }
}

var color = UIColor.errorColor(.API)!
color = UIColor.errorColor(.Normal)!
```

Summary

Now you know how to extend existing types with extensions. You can tell from these simple examples that extensions are very powerful compared to categories in Objective-C. If you look at the source of the Swift standard library, you'll notice that it makes extensive use of extensions. For instance, the Array type has at least eight different extensions. Typically, each extension conforms to a protocol, which makes it easy to factor your code. Also, extensions don't have names as they do in Objective-C, which makes it easier to work with them.

Chapter 15

Memory Management and ARC

Memory management is part of a more general problem in programming called resource management. Every computer system has finite resources for a program to use. These include memory, open files, and network connections. If you use a resource, such as by opening a file, you need to clean up after yourself (in this case, by closing the file). If you keep on opening files but never close them, you'll eventually run out of file capacity. Think about your public library. If everyone borrowed books but never returned them, eventually the library would close because it would have no more books.

Of course, when your program ends, the operating system reclaims the resources it used. But as long as your program is running, it uses resources, and if you don't practice cleanliness, some resource will eventually be used up and your program will probably crash. Moreover, as operating systems evolve, the notion of when a program actually ends is becoming fuzzy.

Not every program uses files or network connections, but every program uses memory. Memory-related errors are the bane of every programmer who uses manual memory management. Our friends in the Java and scripting worlds have it easy: memory management happens automatically for them, like having their parents clean up their rooms. We, on the other hand, have to make sure to allocate memory when we need it and free that memory when we're finished with it. If we allocate without freeing, we'll leak memory: our program's memory consumption will grow and grow until we run out of memory and then the program will crash. We need to be equally careful not to use any memory after we free it. We might be using stale data, which can cause all sorts of errors, or something else might have moved into that memory, and then we end up corrupting the new stuff.

> **Note** Memory management is a difficult problem. Swift's solutions are rather elegant, but it does take some time to wrap your mind around it. Even programmers with decades of experience have problems when first encountering this material, so don't worry if it leaves your head spinning for a while.

Object Life Cycle

Objects within a program have a life cycle. They're born (via new); they live (receive messages and do stuff), make friends (via composition and arguments to methods), and eventually die (get freed) when their lives are over. When that happens, their raw materials (memory) are recycled and used for the next generation. When an object is created, you do so using one of the defined initializers, and when the object is destroyed the deinitializer is called. You can do any work that's required during the creation and destruction of the object.

Reference Counting

Now, it's pretty obvious when an object is born, and we have talked a lot about how to use an object, but how do you know when an object's useful life is over? Swift uses a technique known as reference counting, also sometimes called retain counting. Every object has an count associated with it, known as its reference count or retain count. When some chunk of code is interested in an object, the code increases the object's retain count, saying, "I am interested in this object." When that code is done with the object, it decreases the retain count, indicating that it has lost interest in that object. When the retain count goes to 0, nobody cares about the object anymore so it's destroyed and its memory is returned to the system for reuse.

> **Note** Reference counting only applies to instances of classes, and not to structures or enumeration types. Structures and enumeration types are value types, not reference types. Value types are copied every time they're assigned or passed, so each value object is a distinct item.

Object Ownership

Reference counting doesn't seem hard. What's the big deal? You create an object, use it, release it, and memory management is happy. That doesn't sound terribly complicated, but things get more complex when you factor in the concept of object ownership. When something is said to "own an object," that something is responsible for making sure the object gets cleaned up.

An object with instance variables that point to other objects is said to own those other objects. That's called a strong reference. It means you have a firm hold on that object, and it will not be released until you let go of that hold.

ARC

Automatic **R**eference **C**ounting, or ARC, is a compile-time system that keeps track of and manages the memory an application uses. ARC is pretty smart; most of the time you don't have to worry about allocation and deallocation of memory.

To illustrate how ARC works, let's start by creating a simple class called Student, into which we will put some debug statements so we can see what's going on.

```
class Student {
    let name : String
    init(name : String) {
        self.name = name;
        print("Student \(self.name) is being initialized")
    }

    deinit {
        print("Student \(self.name) is being deinitialized")
    }
}
```

> **Note** If you wish to experiment with this, you can use a playground, which we discussed in Chapter 2. Playground objects remain allocated after their retain count indicates they are no longer used, so they can be examined for debugging. If you want to try these examples, create a command-line tool project and step through it with the debugger.

As you can see, in the init method we print the student's name and a message saying that student is being initialized. And we also added a deinit method so we could print a message when the object goes away.

The following code creates an instance of Student and assigns it to the variable student. Now the variable student has a strong reference.

```
var student : Student? = Student(name: "Adam Malik")
// prints Student Adam Malik is being initialized
```

If we assign a nil to student, we give up the strong reference and the system will reclaim the memory.

```
student = nil
// prints Student Adam Malik is being deinitialized
```

Now let's create some more references to the variable by creating more objects and assigning the existing object to them

```
var student : Student? = Student(name: "Adam Malik")
var student1 : Student? = student
var student2 : Student? = student
```

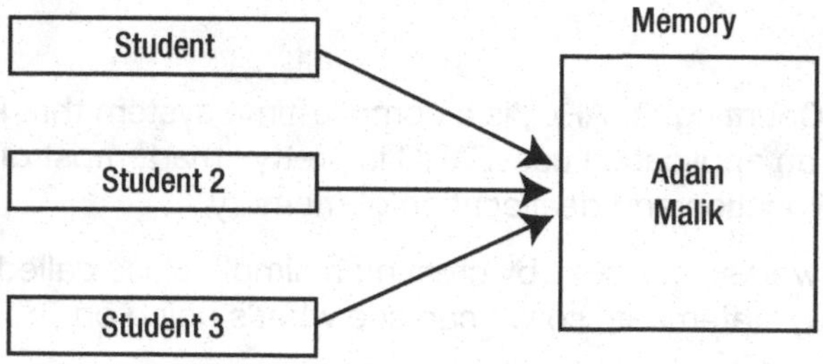

Now there are three strong references to the original object. When we run this program, we don't get a `deinit` message. Even if we assign nil to `student` and `student1`, the object is still not released because `student2` still has a strong reference. However, if we assign nil to all three objects, there are no strong references to the `student` object and the system will release it.

Strong Reference Cycles

The previous example is simple and straightforward and ARC can correctly manage the memory. But most programs you'll write aren't that simple. In the next example we will create two new classes called `Driver` and `Automobile`.

```
class Automobile
{
    let name : String
    init(name: String) {
        self.name = name
    }

    var driver : Driver? = nil;
    deinit {
        print("Automobile \(name) is being deinitialized")
    }
}

class Driver
{
    let name : String
    init(name : String) {
        self.name = name
    }

    var automobile : Automobile? = nil
    deinit {
        print("Driver \(name) is being deinitialized")
    }
}
```

Notice that the Driver type has an optional property called automobile and the Automobile type has an optional property called driver. Let's create a car and a driver. Both of these variables have a strong reference and so far they are independent of each other; if we were to nil them out, they'd just go away.

```
var mario : Driver? = Driver(name: "Mario Andretti")
var ferrari : Automobile? = Automobile(name: "Ferrari")
```

Now let's assign a driver to the automobile instance and an automobile to the driver instance:

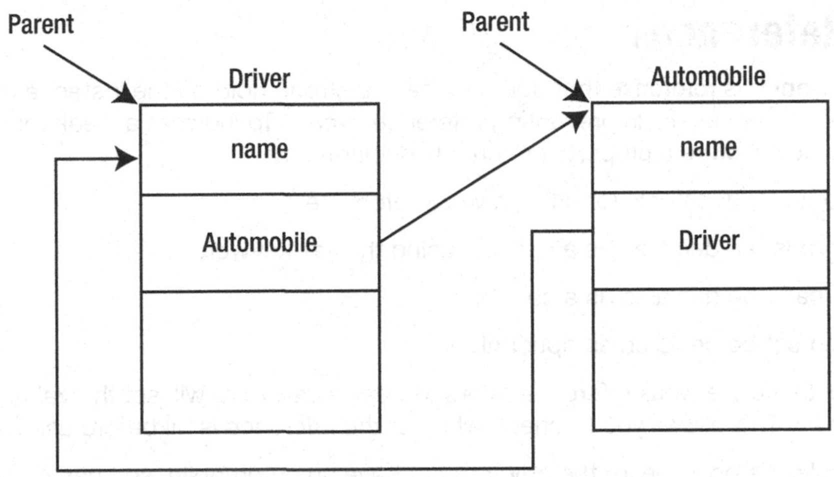


```
mario!.automobile = ferrari
ferrari!.driver = mario
```

By doing this, the Driver instance has a strong reference to the Automobile instance and the Automobile instance has a strong reference to the Driver instance. If we were to nil out the mario object and the ferrari object, unfortunately we wouldn't get deinit messages. Both of these instances have two strong references and by niling the original variables, we only decreased the references by 1. They still have one more reference, and since it is not zero that memory is still in use. This is called a cycle because they hold strong reference to each other. Because we lost the original references, we no longer have access to that memory and now we also have a memory leak.

Resolving Strong Reference Cycles

How can we solve this problem? Swift provides two ways to resolve cycles: weak references and unowned references.

Both of these references enable instances of types to refer to other instances without having a strong hold on them. In this case, the driver and automobile types can refer to each other without having a cycle. What's the difference between these two types of references and when do you use them?

- Use a weak reference whenever it's valid for that reference to become nil at some point during its lifetime.
- Use an unowned reference when you know that the reference will never be nil once it has been set during initialization.

Weak References

A **weak reference** is reference that does not have a strong hold on the instance it refers to. This behavior is very useful in preventing reference cycles. To indicate a weak reference, use the keyword weak before a property or variable declaration.

There are some requirements for using a weak reference:

- It must be declared as a variable using the var keyword.
- It can't be declared as a constant.
- It must be declared as optional.

When the instance the weak reference refers to goes away, ARC will set the value of the reference to nil. This allows you to check whether the reference is nil before using it.

In our example, it's possible for the driver to not have an automobile, so I can declare the automobile property to be weak.

```
class Driver2
{
    let name : String
    init(name : String) {
        self.name = name
    }

    weak var automobile : Automobile2? = nil
    deinit {
        print("Driver \(name) is being deinitialized")
    }
}

class Automobile2
{
    let name : String
    init(name: String) {
        self.name = name
    }
```

```
    var driver : Driver2? = nil
    deinit {
        print("Automobile \(name) is being deinitialized")
    }
}
```

Now we create two instances of the types and assign some values. We have an instance of `Driver2` that has a strong reference. Also, `renault` has a strong reference to the `Automobile2` instance. After we assign some values to the references, we have another strong reference to the `Driver` instance but a weak reference to the `Automobile` instance. When we are done with `driver` and `automobile`, we can get rid of them and ARC will correctly clean up the memory.

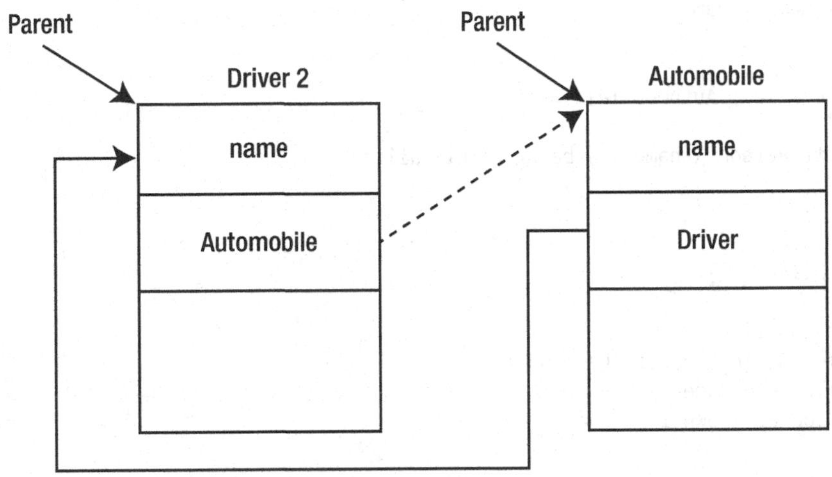


```
var vettel : Driver2? = Driver2(name: "Sebastian Vettel")
var renault : Automobile2? = Automobile2(name: "Renault")
vettel?.automobile = renault
renault?.driver = vettel

renault = nil
vettel = nil
// Automobile Renault is being deinitialized
// Driver Sebastian Vettel is being deinitialized
```

Unowned Reference

Just like weak references, unowned references don't have a strong reference to the instance they refer to. The difference is that an unowned reference must always have a valid value. You define the unowned reference by using the `unowned` keyword. With regard to unowned references

- They can't be declared as optional.
- ARC can't set the value to nil.

If you access the value of an unowned reference after its instance has been deallocated, you'll get a runtime error and your program will crash.

We are going to extend the example. Let's say a `Person` may or may not own an automobile but an automobile must have an owner, so we make the `automobile` property of the `Person` object optional and a weak reference, but the `owner` property of the automobile unowned. Since `Automobile` must have an owner, we have to create an `automobile` by passing the `name` and the `owner` values to the initializer.

```
class Person
{
    let name : String
    init(name : String) {
        self.name = name
    }

    var automobile : Automobile3? = nil
    deinit {
        print("Person \(name) is being deinitialized")
    }
}

class Automobile3
{
    let name : String
    init(name: String, owner: Person) {
        self.name = name
        self.owner = owner
    }

    weak var driver : Person? = nil

 unowned var owner : Person
    deinit {
        print("Automobile \(name) is being deinitialized")
    }
}

var waqar : Person? = Person(name : "Waqar Malik")
var vw : Automobile3? = Automobile3(name: "Volkswagen", owner: waqar!)
waqar?.automobile = vw
```

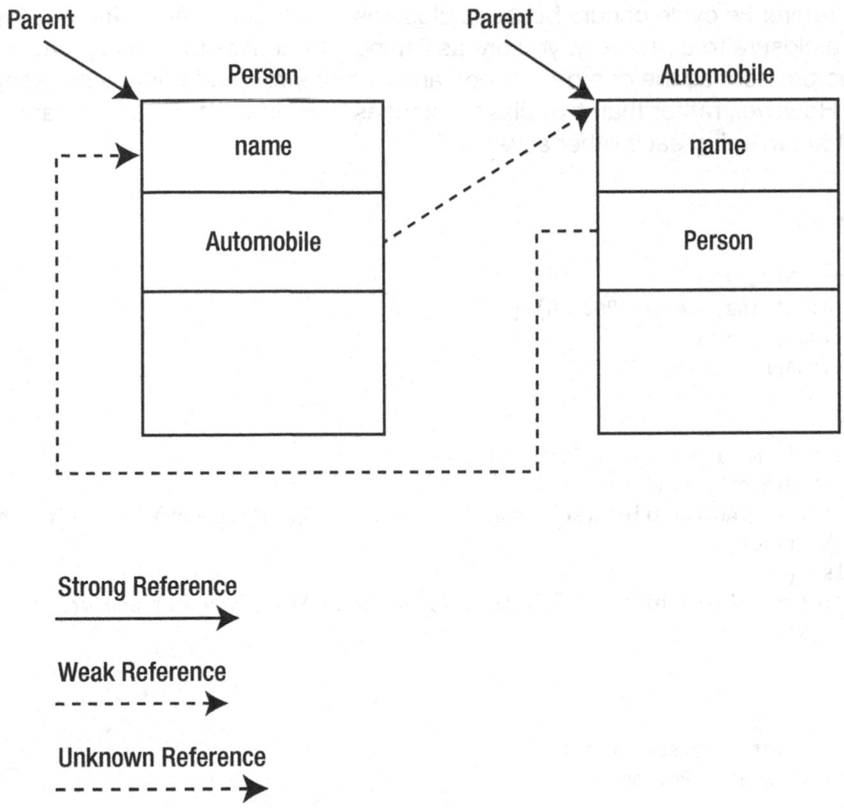

We have a strong reference to `automobile` for `Person`, and a weak reference to `owner`.

Strong Reference Cycles and Closures

You've already seen that having strong references can lead to strong reference cycles where you leak memory. You also know that closures capture the environment around them, which can cause strong reference cycles quite easily.

A strong reference cycle can occur if you assign a closure to a property of a class instance, and the body of that closure captures the instance. This capture might occur because the closure's body accesses a property of the instance, such as `self.someProperty`, or because the closure calls a method on the instance, such as `self.someMethod`. In either case, these accesses cause the closure to "capture" `self`, creating a strong reference cycle.

This strong reference cycle occurs because closures, like classes, are reference types. When you assign a closure to a property, you are assigning a reference to that closure. In essence, it's the same problem as the one described earlier—two strong references are keeping each other alive. However, rather than two class instances, this time it's a class instance and a closure that are keeping each other alive.

```
class Automobile3
{
    let name : String
    init(name: String, owner: Person) {
        self.name = name
        self.owner = owner
    }

    lazy var information : () -> String = {
        if let driver = self.driver {
            return "Automobile \(self.name) is owned by \(self.owner) and driven by
            \(driver)"
        } else {
            return "Automobile \(self.name) is owned by \(self.owner) and driven by
            \(self.owner)"
        }
    }

    weak var driver : Person? = nil
    unowned var owner : Person
    deinit {
        print("Automobile \(name) is being deinitialized")
    }
}
```

This example shows how to create a strong reference cycle when using a closure. The class `Automobile3` defines a `lazy` property called `information`, which combines various other properties and returns a string representation of the automobile. The property `information` is not a regular property; it's a function that takes no arguments and returns a string, `() -> String`, and we are assigning a closure.

The class instance's `information` property holds a strong reference to the closure and the closure references `self` in its body. The closure captures itself, which means the closure has a strong reference to the instance of the class.

> **Note** Even though the closure references `self` multiple times, only one strong reference is captured.

To solve this problem, Swift provides a solution that uses a closure capture list, which defines the rules to use when capturing one or more reference types within the closure's body. As part of the definition of a closure, you can define how to capture the instances you need to use. Use either `unowned` or `weak`, depending how the instances are defined.

To define a capture list, put each reference to a class instance, together with either the `weak` or `unowned` keyword, in square brackets, before the implementation of the closure, like so:

```
{ [capture list] (arguments) -> returnType in
}
```

If you don't have any arguments or a return type for the closure, you can omit those and the syntax looks like this

```
{ [capture list] in
}
```

> **Note** You want to capture `self` as unowned because it should never become nil.

Now that you know how to resolve a strong reference cycle, let's fix that in the example. The only thing I need to change is to add the capture list to the closure:

```
    lazy var information : () -> String = {
        [unowned self] in
        if let driver = self.driver {
            return "Car \(self.name) is owned by \(self.owner) and driven by \(driver)"
        } else {
            return "Car \(self.name) is owned by \(self.owner) and driven by \(self.owner)"
        }
    }
```

In this case, `self` is captured as an `unowned` reference, and the strong reference cycle is broken.

Summary

Managing memory in Swift is a complicated subject. You learned how Swift manages its memory using ARC. If you aren't careful how you define properties on the classes, it can lead to strong reference cycles.

You learned how to break those strong reference cycles, especially when it comes to closures. Even the simplest form of closure can cause a strong reference cycle, and you saw how to avoid those using a capture list.

Chapter 16

Error Handling

What is error handling? It is a process of properly handling unusual conditions in the program. There is an old saying: Garbage in, garbage out. Computers are machines that are very good at processing commands without questioning the input that is given to it. So if you give them bad data (garbage data), they will process it and give you bad results (garbage out). So it is the programmer's responsibility to put guards against invalid or erroneous situations. Swift provides first-class support for handling these situations.

Let's take a situation of downloading data from a remote server. If everything went correct, you would have data and then you could process it, but there can be various errors:

- Network not reachable
- Data Missing
- Do not have permissions to download data
- Corrupted data either on the server or during the download

This list just to name a few of the issues you might have to deal with. You need to know what kind of error happened to correctly recover and continue with the program.

Representing Errors

In Swift, to process errors, they have to conform to the `ErrorType` protocol. It is particularly suited to be used in conjunction with Swift enum types. You can define an enum that conforms to this protocol to group similar errors together. You could define `NetworkError`, `FileError`, or `DataError`, for instance.

```
enum NetworkError : ErrorType {
    case HostUnreachable
    case InvalidPermissions
    case DataMissing
}
```

Now that we have represented the error, how do we report the error? We do that by throwing an error: this tells the runtime that an unusual condition happened, and we specify what the cause of that condition was by specifying the error enum. Use the throw keyword and then error type.

```
throw NetworkError.DataMissing
```

Handling Errors

Now that we have reported an error, you also need code around where the error was thrown to properly handle it and recover from it. There are various ways to process errors: correcting the problem, trying a different approach, or reporting it to the user.

In Swift there are four ways to handle errors:

- Propagate the error to the function callee
- Handle the error using the do-catch block
- Process an error as an optional value
- Assert that errors will not happen

When the error is thrown, the flow of a program is interrupted, and it important to correctly and quickly handle the error and continue the flow of the program. If you know where there is a possibility of an error in the code, you can use the `try` keyword and `catch` to properly catch the error after throwing.

Error handling in Swift looks lot like `@try`, `@catch` block in Objective-C or exception handling in some other languages. In exception handling the stack must be unwound (remove any objects that are no longer needed) to restore the program to a useful state; unwinding the stack is computationally intensive. The compiler has to generate extra code to keep track of what objects must be destroyed or cleaned up when an exception is thrown.

Whereas the `try catch` in Swift is very lightweight, the performance characteristics are the same as return statements. The cost to return from a function is very little: the compiler does not have to generate extra code to destroy an object when an error happens since the compiler has already set up the stack for normal return.

Propagating Errors

When you do not want to or don't know how to handle errors in a function, you can propagate the error to the callee function. Before you can do that you have to let the callee know that you will propagate the error to them. You do that by marking the function with the `throws` keyword before the return type.

```
func functionThatThrows() throws -> Int {
    return 0
}
```

If you do not mark the function with the `throws` keyword, then all errors within the function must be handled and cannot be propagated.

```
func functionThatHandles() -> Int {
    // handle errors

    return 0
}
```

Keep in mind that when you throw an error, the execution of the function stops and returns the control over to the callee scope.

```
import Darwin

enum MathError : ErrorType {
    case DivideByZero
    case NotANumber
}

func divide(a : Double, b : Double) throws -> Double {
    guard b != 0 else {
        throw MathError.DivideByZero
    }

    guard isnan(a) == false && isnan(b) == false else {
        throw MathError.NotANumber
    }

    return a/b
}
```

Let's go over this simple example. First we define two error types, and then we define our method called divide that will take two numbers and does the division. The first thing the function does is to verify that the denominator is not 0 (zero); we know that divide by zero is not defined in mathematics, we cannot divide so we throw the error `MathError.DivideByZero`.

Next we check to make sure that the numbers that are given to us are valid. If either one of those is not a number, we throw another error. We make sure we have a valid number by using the `isnan` function, which tells us if the number is not a number.

Finally, we have everything valid so we return the result by dividing. To call the throwing function, we must use the try key to execute the function:

```
try divide(4.3, b: 2.1)
```

If the callee function also throws an error, and that function does not handle the error, the error will be propagated to its callee function.

```
func function1(a : Double, b : Double) throws {
    // code befores
    try function2(a, y: b)
    // code after
}
```

```
func function2(x :Double, y : Double) throws {
    // code before
    try divide(x, b: y)
    // code after
}
```

This is an extreme example to demonstrate the chain: the function divide throws an error within function2, which in turn does not handle the error. It just passes the error along to function1, which also does not handle the error; and it passes it along to its parent.

Handling Errors

Rather than propagating errors, we can handle and make a decision as to what to do next. You do this by the do-catch block: you wrap the error throwing code around and see if there are any errors; if there are errors they are matched within the catch block and processed. The general form is:

```
do {
  try expression
  statements
} catch pattern1 {
  statements
} catch pattern2 where condition {
  statements
} catch {
  statements
}
```

You must provide one catch statement for each do clause. And if you do not provide any pattern in the catch clause, the catch without any pattern to match will handle all types of errors with a local variable named error. In the general form above, the very last catch will handle any error.

```
do
{
    let result = try divide(4.3, b: 2.1)
} catch MathError.DivideByZero {
    print("The denominator must not be zero")
} catch MathError.NotANumber {
    print("One of the values is not a valid number")
}
```

Or

```
do
{
    let result = try divide(4.3, b: 0)
} catch {
    print(error)
}
```

Optional Handling

Sometime you don't want to handle the errors, either you are not sure what errors will be thrown, or it is not really important if the function fails or succeds, specially when you are only looking for a result returned from a function. In our divide function we really don't care what kind of error is returned we just want to know if it succeds and if the valid value is returned.

We can use the try? keyword to let the compiler know that we don't care what kind of error is thrown. If the function succeeds, return a valid value; if the function fails just return nil. That means that the result returned by the try? is an optional value, and must be handled properly.

```
let result = try? divide(8, b: 2)
let result1 = try? divide(23.9, b: 0)
```

The first statement will try the function, and if it does not throw any errors it will give you a result as an optional value with a valid result. In our case the result will be 4.

The second statement will try the divide function, but we know that since b is zero the function will throw an error; hence the result1 will be nil. the try? Code, which is equivalent to

```
var result2 : Double?
do {
    result2 = try divide(23.9, b: 0)
} catch {
    result2 = nil
}
```

This gives you the option to use the if let pattern.

```
if let result = try? divide(32.9, b: 0) {
        // do something with result
}
```

Asserting Errors

If you know for sure that the throwing function will not throw an error by checking the arguments and only calling the function with valid values, then you can force unbox the result using the try! keyword. If the function does throw an error, then you will get a runtime error and your program will most likely crash.

```
let result4 = try! divide(46.2, b: 12.1)
```

Cleanup Actions

When you are writing a function, you need to clean up some things before you leave the function. Let's say you need to read data from a file and then open the file handle. You start to read the data from it but part way through reading the data, the function throws an error, and you will not be able to close the file handle.

You can use the `defer` statement in this case: The `defer` statement will be executed no matter how you exit the function. It could be either an error thrown or return statement or break statement.

What a defer statement does is that it defers the execution of the code until the current scope of the execution is exited.

The general form of `defer` has one restriction: it must not contain a statement that transfers the control out of the defer block; these include `return` and `break`. That means the defer block must execute all of its code.

```
defer {
  statements
}
```

You can have multiple defer statements in your code:

```
defer {
 // defer1
  statements
}
statements1
defer {
 // defer 2
 statements
}
statements2
```

The order of the execution of defer statements is in reverse when they are defined. If we exit after statements2, then the defer2 statements will be executed first and the defer1 statements will be executed after that.

> **Note** You can use defer statements even if the function is not a throwing function. It's a nice way to clean up resources after the function is done.

Summary

Swift has first-class handling of errors. This is not exception handling in some languages. There is no speed impact to use these patterns. This error handling is also compatible with Cocoa error propagation in Objective-C. You can handle some errors in your functions and propagate some of them out to calling scope. This makes your program readable and stable.

Chapter 17

Protocols

In the real world, people on official business are often required to follow strict procedures when dealing with certain situations. Law enforcement officials, for example, are required to "follow protocol" when making inquiries or collecting evidence.

In the world of object-oriented programming, it's important to be able to define a set of behaviors that's expected of an object in a given situation. As an example, a table view expects to be able to communicate with a data source object in order to find out what it's required to display. This means the data source must be able to respond to the specific messages the table view might send.

Protocols define the interface—a blueprint of methods, properties, and other requirements for a specific task. The protocol does not actually implement the functionality itself, it only describes the implementation. In Java they are called interfaces.

Any object that implements the requirements a protocol describes is said to **conform** to the protocol. A protocol can require a specific instance of the type to have:

- Properties
- Instance methods
- Type methods
- Operators
- Subscripts

Syntax

You define a protocol in the same way you define classes, structures, and enumeration types:

```
protocol SomeProtocol {
    // Your protocol requirements
}
```

Your protocol can also inherit from another protocol:

```
protocol SomeProtocol : NSObjectProtocol {
    // Your protocol requirements
}
```

In Objective-C you could have a protocol and class with the same name, such as class `NSObject` and protocol `NSObject`, but in Swift the names can't be the same. In the preceding example, the protocol inherits from `NSObjectProtocol`, which is the same as `NSObject` protocol in Objective-C.

When a type conforms to one or more protocols, you define that type by giving the list of protocols after the colon separator, and you can list multiple protocols using the comma separator:

```
struct SomeStruct : SomeProtocol, AnotherProtocol {
        // your implementation of structure
}
```

If your class has a parent class, you can list the protocols after the parent class:

```
class SomeClass : ParentClass, SomeProtocol, AnotherProtocol {
        // your implementation of class
}
```

Properties

Protocols can require the implementing type (or conforming type) to provide a property that can be either gettable (read-only) or settable and gettable (read-write). The protocol doesn't specify that the specific property has to be stored or computed; the implementing type can implement the property as it likes as long as it conforms to the protocol interface.

If the property is settable, it can't be either a constant stored or gettable computed property. Only gettable properties can be used to satisfy any requirements.

Property requirements are always defined as `var`, not `let`. You define the property as either read-only or read-write by adding either the `get` function or both `get` and `set` functions in braces after the type declaration.

```
protocol SomeProtocol {
    // Your protocol requirements
    var readwriteProperty : Int { set get}
    var readonlyProperty : Int { get }
}
```

To define a type property, you prefix the property with the `class` keyword, even when you use the protocol for structures and enumerations.

> **Note** This rule applies to structures and enumeration types where you use the static keyword.

```
protocol AnotherProtocol {
    static var typeProperty : Int { get set }
}
struct SomeStruct : SomeProtocol, AnotherProtocol {
    var readwriteProperty : Int
    private(set) var readonlyProperty : Int
    static var typeProperty : Int {
        get {
        return 0
        }

        set {

        }
    }
}
```

That was a simple example showing how to conform a structure to your protocols. But it doesn't really help us; let's look at a concrete example of how this works:

```
protocol FullName {
    var fullName : String { get }
}

struct Person : FullName {
    var lastName : String
    var firstName : String
    var middleName : String?

    init (firstName : String, lastName : String) {
        self.lastName = lastName
        self.firstName = firstName
    }

    var fullName : String {
        return firstName + (middleName == nil ? "" : " " + middleName!) + " " + lastName
    }
}

var alan = Person(firstName: "Alan", lastName: "Turing")
print(alan.fullName)
alan.middleName = "Mathison"
print(alan.fullName)
```

Methods

The most common requirements for a protocol are specific instance and type methods. You define the methods in a protocol as you'd define them in a type but without the implementation, that is, without the curly braces.

> **Note** When defining a method requirement, you can't specify default values for method parameters.

Similar to the property requirement, you use the keyword `class` when defining type methods, even when they are implemented in structures and enumerations with the `static` keyword.

The following example shows a protocol that requires two methods: an instance method and a type method. Neither of these methods takes any arguments or has a return value.

```
protocol MethodProtocol {
    func instanceMethod ()
    static func typeMethod ()
}
```

If your methods will modify the state of a structure or enumeration type, you have to specify that with the `mutating` keyword:

```
protocol MethodProtocol {
    mutating func instanceMethod ()
    static func typeMethod ()
}
```

Initializers

Protocols can require a specific initializer to be implemented by a conforming class. You define these initializers in the protocol just as with regular initializers, but without the curly braces.

```
protocol SomeProtocol {
    init(parameter : Double)
}
```

The conforming class can implement these as either convenience or designated initializers. In either case the implementation of the initializer must be marked using the `required` modifier.

```
class SomeClass : SomeProtocol {
    required init(parameter: Double) {
    }
}
```

The required modifier is necessary to ensure that the conforming class provides an explicit or inherited implementation of the initializer on all of its subclasses so they conform to the protocol as well.

> **Note** You don't need to provide the `required` keyword for an initializer if the class is marked as `final`.

If the subclass overrides a designated initializer and also implements the matching initializer requirements from a protocol, then both the required and override keywords must be used to properly satisfy both requirements.

```
class ParentClass {
    init(parameter : Double) {
    }
}

class SomeClass : ParentClass, SomeProtocol {
    required override init(parameter: Double) {
        super.init()
    }
}
```

You can also require failable initializers in your protocol. A failable initializer requirement can be satisfied by either a failable or nonfailable initializer. For a nonfailable initializer, you can use a failable initializer and explicitly unwrap it.

Protocols as Types

When you define a protocol, it becomes a type that can be used much like any other type, even though the protocol doesn't provide its own implementation.

Protocol types can be used as:

- Parameter types for methods.
- Return types for methods.
- A type for a constant, variable, or property.
- A type for an item in an array, dictionary, or other container.

```
class SomeClass {
    var protocolConformingProperty : SomeProtocol
    init(someObject : SomeProtocol) {
        self.protocolConformingProperty = someObject
    }
}
var myClass = SomeClass (someObject: SomeStruct(readwriteProperty: 5, readonlyProperty: 10))
print(myClass.protocolConformingProperty.readonlyProperty)
```

In this example, SomeClass has a property that conforms to a protocol, and the init method has the object that the class is initialized with as the same protocol type.

Delegation

If you've been an iOS or OS X developer for any length of time, you've no doubt used table views, which have one property called delegate. Delegate is a design pattern that delegates or offloads some of the work to an instance of another type that's better suited to it. The delegate property is defined as conforming to a given protocol.

The following example defines a simple protocol for a download manager. It defines two methods to start and end a download.

> **Note** If you need to use any Objective-C protocol as a base protocol, you will need to import the appropriate module where the parent protocol is defined. In our case we need to import Foundation module.

```
import Foundation
public protocol DownloadManagerDelegate : NSObjectProtocol {
    func downloadManagerDidStart(manager : DownloadManager)
    func downloadManagerDidEnd(manager : DownloadManager)
}

public class DownloadManager
{
    public weak var delegate : DownloadManagerDelegate?

    init() {
        print("init")
    }

    public func GET(path : String, parameters : [String : AnyObject]? = nil) {
        self.delegate?.downloadManagerDidStart(self)
        // do your work
        self.delegate?.downloadManagerDidEnd(self)
    }
}
```

The view controller will adopt the protocol to keep track of the start and end of the network calls we will be making. To use it in the controller we need to implement the required methods:

> **Note** Since we are using UIViewController you must import UIKit module before you can use this class.

```
class ViewController: UIViewController, DownloadManagerDelegate
{
    private var downloadManager : DownloadManager?

    override func viewDidLoad() {
        super.viewDidLoad()
        // Do any additional setup after loading the view, typically from a nib.
        self.downloadManager = DownloadManager()
        self.downloadManager?.delegate = self

        self.downloadManager?.GET("/articles")
    }
```

```
    func downloadManagerDidStart(manager: DownloadManager) {
        print("Download did start.")
    }

    func downloadManagerDidEnd(manager: DownloadManager) {
        print("Download did finish.")
    }
}
```

Conformance with Extensions

If you have an existing type that you'd like to conform to a protocol, you can do that by implementing the protocol requirements in the extension.

Protocols can be extended to provide method or property implementations to conforming types. This is done at the protocol level and not at each conforming type.

> **Note** Apple calls this Protocol-Oriented Programming.

What this provides is that any type that is conforming to the extended protocol will get an extension as part of the conformance. To extend a protocol the syntax is the same as extending other types such as class or structure.

```
extension ProtocolType {
// protocol extension implemention
}
```

Now any other type that conforms to this protocol will get that method. In Swift the collection types conform to the protocol called `CollectionType`; we can extend this protocol to add a method.

```
extension CollectionType {
    func printAll() {
        print("\(self)")
    }
}

var myArray : Array<String> = ["a", "b"]

myArray.printAll()

var myDictionary : Dictionary<String,String> = ["ca" : "California", "tx" : "Texas"]
myDictionary.printAll()
```

Now any type that conforms to `CollectionType` will get our new method.

Protocols and Collection Types

A protocol type can be a member of a collection type, such as an array or dictionary. As you know, once a protocol is defined it becomes a first-class type object, and you can simply use it in place of values:

```
protocol SomeProtcol {
    func someFunction()
}

class MyOject1 : SomeProtcol {
    func someFunction() {
        print("someFunction")
    }
}

class MyOject2 : SomeProtcol {
    func someFunction() {
        print("someFunction")
    }
}

let object1 = MyOject1()
let object2 = MyOject2()
let items : [SomeProtcol] = [object1, object2]
```

This example shows that `items` is a collection of objects that conform to `SomeProtocol`; this is one way to store heterogeneous objects. Objects don't have to be of the same type as long as they conform to the protocol you want.

Protocol Inheritance

Protocols can inherit from one or more parent protocols, as you saw with the `DownloadManagerDelegate` protocol that inherits from `NSObjectProtocol`. The syntax is similar to that of class inheritance, but allows listing of multiple parent protocols.

```
protocol SomeProtocol : ParentProtocol {
}

protocol SomeOtherProtocol : ParentProtocol, AnotherParentProtocol {
}
```

You can limit the protocol to be used with classes only, and not structures or enumerations, by adding the `class` keyword before the list of parent protocols. Both of the following examples limit the use `MyProtocol` to reference types and not value types:

```
protocol MyProtocol : class {
}
protocol MyProtocol : class, NSObjectProtocol {
}
```

Protocol Composition

Sometimes you want to be able to require a type to conform to multiple protocols. Swift provides a protocol composition construct that lets you do this. Instead of using the protocol type as the type of the variable, you replace it with a composition having the format `protocol<SomeProtocol, AnotherProtocol>`, which will create a temporary local protocol that combines all the listed protocols.

```
func myFunction(parameter : protocol <SomeProtocol, AnotherProtocol>) {
}
```

This function's parameter is required to conform to all of the protocols. In this case, if the instance of the type doesn't conform to both protocols it will be rejected.

Protocol Conformance

You can use the `is` as an `as` operator to check for protocol conformance. It is used exactly the same way the casting syntax is used.

The `is` operator returns true or false depending on if the object conforms to or not conforms to the protocol. The as? operator will return an object of the protocol type or nil if the object does not conform to the protocol.

The `as!` operator will force the conversion of the protocol type to another type. If the object does not conform to the protocol; it will be a runtime error and your program will crash.

Optional Requirements

If you have a protocol where not all properties or methods need to be implemented, you can mark those items with the `optional` keyword. When using the optional keyword for methods, the method itself is marked as optional and not the return value. Which means you don't need to implement that method for conformance.

To use the optional keyword, the protocol must be marked with `@objc`, which exposes your protocols to Objective-C runtime even if you do not intend to use it in Objective-C code.

Summary

In this chapter, we introduced the concept of protocols. You define a protocol by listing a set of methods inside a protocol block. Objects adopt this protocol by including the protocol name after the colon when defining a type. When an object adopts a formal protocol, it promises to implement every required method that's listed in the protocol. The compiler helps you keep your promise by giving you an error if you don't implement all the protocol's required methods or properties.

Chapter 18

Generics

Generics are one of the most powerful aspects of the Swift language. If you are coming from Objective-C, this is a new concept, and it might take some getting used to. The main purpose of generics is to enable the writing of adaptable, reusable code.

Generic Functions

Let's take a look at a simple function that compares two integers. The function takes two arguments of type `Int` and returns a Boolean `true` if two values are the same.

```
func equalInts(a : Int, b : Int) -> Bool {
    return a == b
}
```

What if you want to compare two double values or strings? You have to write two new functions:

```
func equalDoubles(a : Double, b : Double) -> Bool {
    return a == b
}

func equalStings(a : String, b : String) -> Bool {
    return a == b
}
```

In all three functions, the implementations are identical. The only difference is the type of the arguments they take. It would be really useful and more flexible to write one function that could compare two values and return the proper result. Generics allow you to do that. Let's write a generic function that lets you compare any type and return the proper result.

To define a function that takes generic values, you create a generic type, which will be replaced by the actual type when you use the function—you put the generic type at the end of the function name in angle brackets and replace the actual types with the generic types in the arguments.

```
func someFunction<T>(argument : T)
```

> **Note** We will use T, short for type, for this generic type. You can use anything as long as it's not an existing type. Also, it's recommended that you use the same convention as naming the types.

The preceding function definition tells the compiler that we have a placeholder type and the argument is of that type, and we will replace the placeholder with the actual type every time this function is called.

When you call the function, you don't need to use the angle brackets:

```
var a : Int = 5
func someFunction(a)
```

The complier will infer the type of the placeholder to be the `Int` type. If we call this function with a type of `Double`, the compiler will infer the placeholder type to be `Double`.

To implement the values equal function, we simply replace the type with the generic:

```
func areValuesEqual<T>(a : T, b: T) -> Bool {
    return a == b
}
```

But we are not quite done yet. If you try to implement the function like it this, the compiler will give you a compile error because the compiler doesn't know how to compare two generic types. It's easy to do that for `Int`, `Double`, and `String`, but what if you're using a custom type? You need to limit the function to any type that implements the == operator, which is defined in the `Equatable` protocol.

```
func areValuesEqual<T : Equatable>(a : T, b: T) -> Bool {
    return a == b
}
```

Now we are set; the generic type T conforms to the `Equatable` protocol. We can tell if two instances of the object are the same as long as they implement the `Equatable` protocol. And we know that numeric and string types conform to the Equatable protocol.

```
let a : Int = 4
let b : Int = 3
let c : Int = 3
areValuesEqual(a, b)
areValuesEqual(b, c)

areValuesEqual1 , 1)
areValuesEqual(2.3, 2.4)
```

The generic type is not limited to arguments. It can also be a return type. And it can be used inside a function to declare new variables of the given type:

```
func areValuesEqual<T : Equatable>(a : T, b: T) -> Bool {
    let localVarible : T = a
    return localVarible == b
}

func someFunction<T>(values : [T]) -> T {
        // implementation
}
```

If you want two generic types of arguments, you can simply add another type to the list:

```
func someFunction<T1, T2>(t2 : T2, t1 : T1)
```

In the preceding example, we narrowed down the types the function can handle. This is called *type constraint*. The general form of type constraint is just adding the class or protocol name after the type, separated by a colon:

```
func someFunction<Type1 : SomeClass, Type2 : SomeProtocol>(arugment1 : Type2, argument2 :
Type1) {
}
```

This function has two arguments: one of type `SomeClass` (or derived from it) and the other conforming to the protocol `SomeProtocol`.

Generic Types

In Chapter 10 we used a `Stack` type. The implementation only worked with the `Double` type. If we wanted to use it for some other type, we have to implement another version. Sometimes it's not possible to know the type of data you'll be using. Imagine a new data type that a user defined that would like to use your stack implementation. That's not possible because we haven't provided an implementation for the user's custom type. Let's take a look at the original implementation.

```
struct DoubleStack {
    private var stack = [Double]()

    func empty () -> Bool {
        print("Stack Empty")
        return stack.count == 0
    }

    func peek () -> Double? {
        return stack.last
    }
```

```
    mutating func pop () -> Double? {
        guard let value = stack.last else {
            return nil
        }
        stack.removeLast()
        return value
    }

    mutating func push (item : Double) {
        stack.append(item)
    }
}
```

Since this implementation works only with `Double` type, if we wanted to store other types we would have to implement a stack type for each of the types we wanted to use. Let's implement a generic version. The syntax is similar to the generic function:

```
struct Stack<Element> {
    private var stack = [Element]()

    func empty () -> Bool {
        print("Stack Empty")
        return stack.count == 0
    }

    func peek () -> Element? {
        return stack.last
    }

    mutating func pop () -> Element? {
        guard let value = stack.last else {
            return nil
        }
        stack.removeLast()
        return value
    }

    mutating func push (item : Element) {
        stack.append(item)
    }
}
```

The generic version is almost the same; we added the generic type to the name of the type. We replaced the `Double` type with my generic type. To use the generic type is a little different because the type can't be inferred. If we want to use the generic type for integers, we have to tell the compiler when we are creating an instance of the stack, and we do that by replacing the generic type with the actual type.

```
var intStack = Stack<Int>()
var stringStack = Stack<String>()
```

The first example creates a stack of `Int` types and the second of `String` types. You can even create a stack for your own types if you wanted to. In the following example, we create a new type called `MyClass`, which lets us create a stack that will hold instances of our new type.

```
class MyClass {
}

var myClassStack = Stack<MyClass>()
```

Extensions

When extending a generic type, you do not need to specify the generic type again in the extension; the original generic type is available.

```
extension Stack<Element> { // Error
}

extension Stack {
    var size : Int {
        get {
            return self.stack.count
        }
    }

    var top : Element? {
        get {
            return self.stack.isEmpty ? nil : self.stack[self.size - 1]
        }
    }
}
```

Associated Types

If you want to define a protocol that needs to use a generic type, you might assume you could do something like this:

```
protocol SomeProtocol<T> {
}
```

You can't, but there is a solution. It's called an *associated type*. An associated type gives a placeholder name (or alias) to a type that's used as part of a protocol. That type will not be defined until the protocol is adopted. To do this you use the `typealias` keyword:

```
protocol SomeProtocol {
        typealias GenericType
}
```

In this example, we define an associated type called GenericType. Now we can use this where we need an actual type. If we were to add a function requirement for this protocol that took an argument whose type will be defined when the protocol is adopted, we would write it as:

```
protocol SomeProtocol {
    typealias GenericType
    func someFunction(argument : GenericType)
}
```

And when a type adopts the protocol, the type has to set the type of the generic type:

```
class SomeClass : SomeProtocol {
    typealias GenericType = Int
    func someFunction(argument: GenericType) {
        // do your processing
    }
}
```

The class SomeClass will adopt the protocol. The first thing we do is set the type of the GenericType by defining it as an Int. Now, in the class where GenericType is used, the compiler will substitute Int for it.

Because Swift has type inference, we don't need to explicitly tell the compiler what GenericType is if we just use Int instead of GenericType as the argument type for someFunction.

```
class SomeClass : SomeProtocol {
    func someFunction(argument: Int) {
        // do your processing
    }
}
```

Now we will create a protocol called Collection, which we can use for arrays, lists, stacks, or any kind of collection. What is common for these types?

- The number of items in the collection
- Adding an item to the collection
- Getting an item from the collection

Using an associated type, we can define a generic protocol to have three functions that might look like this:

```
protocol SpecialCollection {
    typealias SpecialCollectionType
    func count() -> Int
    mutating func add(item : SpecialCollectionType)
    subscript(index : Int) -> SpecialCollectionType { get }
}
```

The following shows what the new version of the stack type would look like. We don't have to explicitly state the type for the SpecialCollectionType protocol; it is inferred by the type system from the add function.

```
struct Stack<T> : SpecialCollection {
    private var stack = [T]()

    func empty () -> Bool {
        print("Stack Empty")
        return stack.count == 0
    }

    func peek () -> T? {
        return stack.last
    }

    mutating func pop () -> T? {
        let value = stack.last
        if nil != value {
            stack.removeLast()
        }
        return value
    }

    mutating func push (item : T) {
        stack.append(item)
    }

    // MARK - SpecialCollection Protocol
    func count() -> Int {
        return self.stack.count
    }

    mutating func add(item: T) {
        self.push(item)
    }

    subscript(index : Int) -> T {
        return self.stack[index]
    }
}
```

Suppose you want to compare two collections and see if the items in the collection are the same. If you have two stack types, you could write an operator on the type and simply compare those.

What if you have two different types, a stack and a list, both of which conform to the SpecialCollection protocol? You'd have to write an operator for stack that compares against a list, and you'd also have to write an operator on the list type that would compare against the stack type. That's lots of duplicate code. Moreover, if you decide to write another type that also conforms to the SpecialCollection protocol, you then have to write the same code for every type you use. That would produce an exponentially large set of duplicate code. The best approach is to write a global function that take two collection types, compare them, and returns a true or false.

```
func areIdentical<T1 : SpecialCollection, T2 : SpecialCollection >(collection1 : T1,
collection2 : T2) -> Bool
```

To implement this function and have it return the correct result involves certain requirements:

1. T1 and T2 must conform to the `SpecialCollection` protocol.
2. Types in the collection must be the same.
3. Types must be comparable.
4. There must be the same number of items.
5. Each item must be in the same order.

You could just implement the method and check for items at runtime, but what if you could do that at compile time? Swift provides a mechanism called a `where` clause. When you define a function, you put the `where` clause after the type requirements. The general form is, just like with types; each clause is separated by a comma:

```
func myFunction<Type1, Type1 where Clause1, Clause2> (arguments) -> ReturnType
```

Here's the updated function definition:

```
func areIdentical<T1 : SpecialCollection, T2 : SpecialCollection
    where T1.SpecialCollectionType == T2.SpecialCollectionType, T1.SpecialCollectionType :
    Equatable>
    (collection1 : T1, collection2 : T2) -> Bool
```

The first clause enforces that types of the collection must be the same, and the second clause enforces that T1 must conform to `Equatable` protocol, which in turn enforces that T2 must also be equatable.

Now the implementation of the function becomes really easy—all we have to do is make sure that the number of items are the same and that each item is the same.

```
func areIdentical<T1 : SpecialCollection, T2 : SpecialCollection

where T1.SpecialCollectionType == T2.SpecialCollectionType, T1.SpecialCollectionType :
Equatable, T2.SpecialCollectionType : Equatable>
    (collection1 : T1, collection2 : T2) -> Bool {
        guard collection1.count() == collection2.count() else {
            return false
        }
```

```
        var areEqual = true
        for index in 0 ..< collection1.count() {
            if collection1[index] != collection2[index] {
                areEqual = false
                break
            }
        }
        return areEqual
}
```

Summary

Whoa, that's lots of new stuff! Generics are one of the features that make Swift a very powerful language and a big departure from Objective-C. In Objective-C, all objects are derived from a single base class called `NSObject`, so every object is of type `NSObject`. In Swift, you can have objects that don't have parent classes, which brings about the need for generics. Now you can write less code by making your code generic; and that, in turn, means fewer bugs.

Chapter 19

Access Control

Access control is a feature of programming languages that restricts access to code based on where it's defined. You can apply access control to the following items:

- Classes
- Structures
- Enumerations
- Properties
- Initializers
- Methods

Some limited support for access control is available for:

- Protocols
- Global functions
- Global constants and variables

Most of the time, you won't have to specify the access level. Swift provides a default access level that works in most cases.

Modules and Source Files

First, we are going to introduce a few terms, because to some extent the access control you get depends on how the code is structured. Access control applies at the module and source file level.

A source file in Swift is a single file (`.swift`) in which you implement your code. Typically, you create a source file for each type (class, struct, and so forth), but you can create multiple types, functions, and more in a single file.

A module in Swift is a set of files compiled into a single executable, which may be either a framework or an application. For example, if you create an iOS/OS X application that consists of multiple files and compile those files into one executable, that's a module. You can also take code that's common among multiple applications and create a framework that can be imported into your application using the `import` keyword, that is another module

Access Levels

Swift provides three levels of access control, from least restrictive to most restrictive:

- *Public* access allows access between modules. If, for example, you are creating a framework and you use public types and methods, anybody who imports your module can use these.
- *Internal* access allows access within a given module. This is the default level if you don't specify the access level explicitly.
- *Private* access allows access only within a given file. This is typically used to hide the implementation details of entities (that is, properties, types, functions, and so forth).

From one entity, you can only define subentities with a more restrictive access level.

- You can't define a public class that has a parent class that's internal or private. But you can define a class that's private from a public or internal class.
- You can't define a public property on a class that's declared as internal or private.
- Functions can't have a more restrictive access level than their arguments or return values.

> **Note** Some languages, like C++ and Java, have an access level called protected. Swift doesn't provide protected access. C++ also has private and public access levels.

Syntax

Swift has three keywords that can be used to define the access level: `private`, `internal`, and `public`.

```
public class MyPublicClass {}
internal class MyInternalClass {}
private class MyPrivateClass {}

public var myPublicVariable = 0
internal let myInternalConstant = 1
private func MyPrivteFunction() {}
```

If you leave out the `internal` keyword, the compiler will give default access level of `internal`.

Classes

You have to give the access level of a class as part of its definition, and this access control affects the class's properties, methods, subscripts, and initializers.

```
private class MyPrivateClass // explicitly private
{
    var myProperty = 0 // implicitly private

    func MyFunction() { // implicitly private

    }
}

class MyInternalClass // explicitly internal
{
    var myInternalProperty = 0  // implicitly internal
    internal var myOtherInternalProperty = 5 // explicitly internal
    private var myPrivateProperty = 4 // explicitly private

    func MyInternalMethod() { // implicitly internal
    }

    private func MyPrivateFunction () { // explicitly private
    }
}

public class MyPublicClass { // explicitly public
    var myPublicProperty = 9 // implicitly internal
    public var myProperty = 7 // explicitly public
    internal var myInternalProperty = 8 // explicitly internal
    private var myPrivateProperty = 5 // explicitly private

    func myFunc1() { // implicitly public
    }

    public func myFunc2 () { // explicitly public
    }

    internal func myFunc3 () { // explicitly internal
    }

    private func myFunc4() { // explicitly private
    }
}
```

Subclassing

You can only subclass parent classes that are visible within your current context. All subclasses of a parent class must have an access control level equal to or stricter than that of the parent. You can't subclass a `public` or `internal` class from a `private` parent class. Furthermore, you can only override class members (methods, properties, subscripts, and initializers) that are visible in a certain context.

```
public class MyOtherClass : MyPublicClass {
    public override func myFunc3 () {
    }

    internal override func myFunc4() {
    }
}
```

Class Members

Constants, properties, subscripts, and variables can't have a higher access level than that of the type they're declared in. You can't define a public property for a private class. A subscript can't be more public than its index type or the return type. If one of these entities makes use of a private type, that entity must also be marked as private.

```
private var myPrivateVar = MyPrivateClass()
```

Functions

The access level for the function is calculated from the function's parameters and return types, using the most restrictive level.

```
func MyFunction () -> (SomePublicType, SomePrivateType) {
// return a tuple
}
```

Since we didn't specify an explicit access level for this function, you'd assume the default level of `internal` would be assigned. But that's not case, because the return value of the function is a `tuple` composed of two distinct types. One type is defined with public access and the other with private, so the overall access level of the tuple is private. Since the return type of the function is private, the function must be declared as private.

```
private func MyFunction () -> (SomePublicType, SomePrivateType) {
// return a tuple
}
```

If you try to declare the function explicity other than private the compiler will give a compile time error and not compile your source file.

Enumerations

The case types for enumerations get the same access level as the enumeration and can't be changed.

```
public enum MyEnum {
    case Left
    case Right
}
```

The access level for .Left and .Right are implicitly public and can't be changed to private or internal.

The types used by the raw values in an enumeration must have an access level as high as the enumeration's. If the enumeration has an access level of internal, you can't use a private access level for raw types, but you can use an internal or public access level.

Nested Types

Nested types defined within a private type are automatically private, but types defined within public or internal types are always internal. If you need to have private access to a type defined in a public type, you have to explicitly mark theitem as such.

```
public class MyPublicClass { // explicitly public
    class MyInnerClass { // implicitly internal
    }
}

public class MyPublicClass { // explicitly public
    public class MyInnerClass { // explicitly public
    }
}
public class MyPublicClass {
    private class MyInnerClass {
        func myInnterFunction() {
            print("Inner Function")
        }
    }
    func myFunction() {
        print("myFunction")
        myInnerClass.myInnterFunction()
    }
    private var myInnerClass = MyInnerClass()
}
```

You cannot create a public instance of MyInnerClass.

Getters and Setters

Getters and setters by default get the same access level as the member they belong to. If you have a public property, for example, the getter and setter will also have public access levels.

You can give a setter stricter access than the getter, if you want to make a read-only property, for example.

```
public private(set) var myPublicProperty = 9
```

This gives the setter private access and the getter as public access.

> **Note** This rule applies to both computed and stored properties.

Initializers

Custom initializers can be defined with an access level less than or equal to the type they are initializing. The only exception is the required initializer must have the same access level as the class it belongs to. Also, the parameters for the initializer can't be more private than the initializer itself.

Swift provides a default initializer (an initializer without any arguments) if you don't define at least one initializer for the type. The default initializer will have the same access level as the type it initializes, unless the type is public. If the type is defined as public, the default initializer is defined as internal. If you want to give explicit public access, you must define a no-arguments initializer with a public access level as part of the type definition.

Protocols

You can assign an access level at the time you define a protocol, so the protocol can only be accessed for a given context. The access level of each item within the protocol is set to the same level as the protocol itself, and the access level can't be changed for these items. When the protocol is implemented, the items receive the access level that was defined for the protocol.

If a protocol inherits from another protocol, the new protocol can have at most the same level as its parent. If a protocol inherits from an internal protocol, for example, you can't implement a public subprotocol; it must be private or internal.

A type can conform to a protocol that has a lower access level than the type itself, so an internal class can implement a public protocol. If you have a public type that implements an internal protocol, only internal types can be used in the module where the protocol is defined.

Extensions

When you extend a class, structure, or enumeration, the access level of the extension defaults to the same level as that of the original type. If you're extending a public type, then all types in the extension will have internal access. You can extend types using an explicit access level. For example, if you want to extend a public class to have just a private extension, you can do so using the private access level `private extension`. You can also set the access level for each member of the type.

> **Note** You can't provide an explicit access level if you're implementing a protocol in an extension. In that case, the access level of the protocol is used.

Type Alias

Type aliases will have an access level less than or equal to the type it is being used to alias. You can make a private or internal alias of a public type, but you can't make a public alias for an internal or private type.

Summary

You learned how to properly allow access to the types you define or when you extend existing types. When in doubt, think of a security-clearance model where a lower level of clearance can't access a higher level of security. In Swift, private is the highest level of protection and public means no protection at all.

Chapter 20

Interoperability with Objective-C

Swift is an awesome language and works great by itself, but when you're writing iOS or OSX applications, you have to interface with the frameworks that Apple provides and perhaps with your own existing frameworks. You may be able to rewrite your own frameworks in Swift, but Apple has not rewritten its frameworks in Swift yet, if it ever will. Apple does provide interoperability with existing frameworks that use the Objective-C and C APIs.

Note Interoperability in this case is the capability of interaction between the Swift and Objective-C APIs in either direction. This means being able to use the Swift API in Objective-C code and the Objective-C API in Swift code.

To use Swift in Objective-C or vice versa, you need to set up the project so you can mix and match these languages properly. Let's start by creating a new Swift project. Start Xcode if you haven't already started it. You can select the new project either from the welcome window or from File ➤ New ➤ Project...(⇧⌘N). I'm going to start with an iOS Single View Application (Figure 20-1).

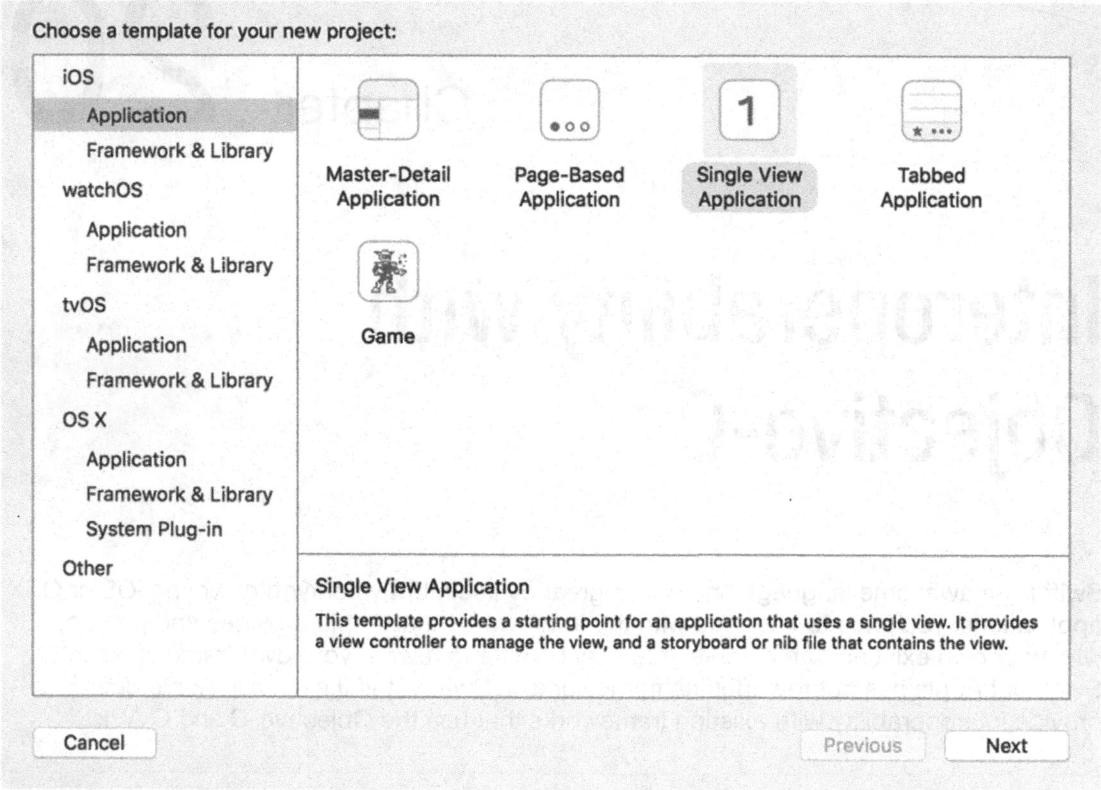

***Figure 20-1.** Choosing a new project template*

Once you've selected the project, click the Next button to get the Project settings window (Figure 20-2). Enter the project name and make sure to select Swift as the language. Now you're ready to experiment.

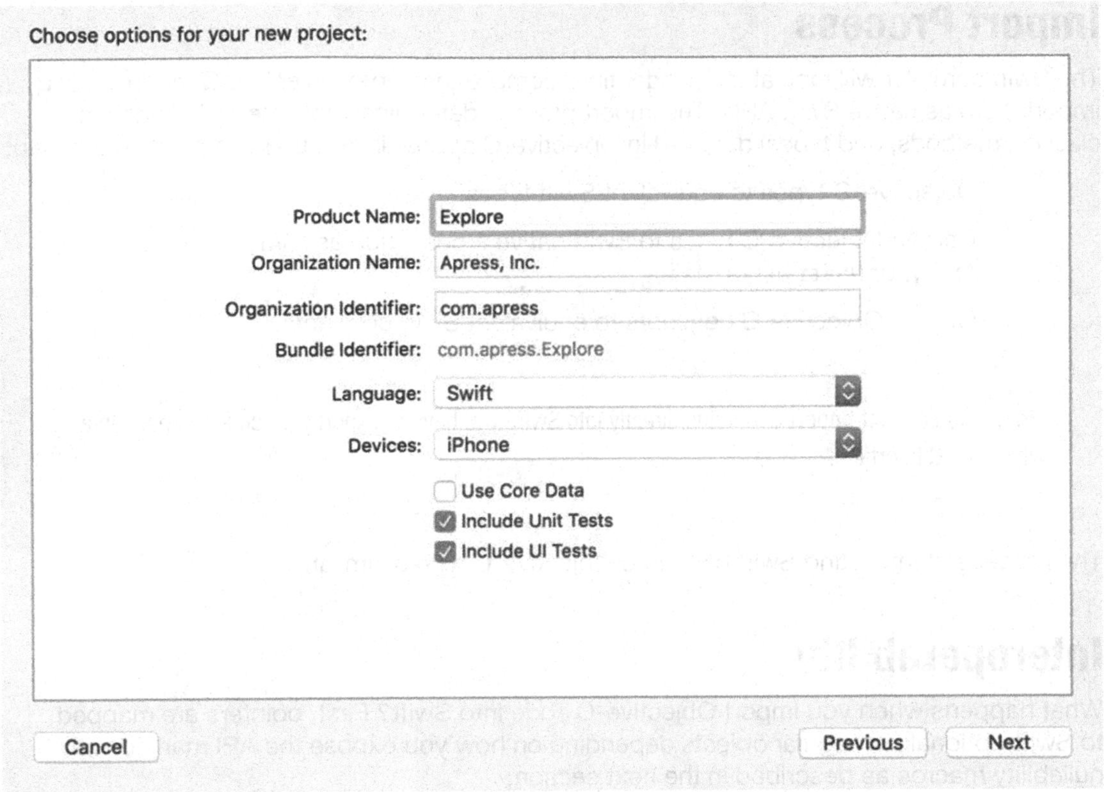

Figure 20-2. Project settings window

If you look at the project explorer, you'll see a couple of Swift files already in your project. Let's look at the `ViewController.swift` file.

> **Note** Unlike Objective-C/C/C++, Swift doesn't use header files; the implementation and interface reside in the same dot Swift file.

After the comments in the file you'll see the `import UIKit` declaration, which tells the Swift compiler you'd like to use the UIKit framework. In Objective-C you'd use either `#import <UIKit/UIKit.h>` or `@import UIKit` to accomplish the same thing. In Swift they are called modules and you use the `import UIKit` to import the module.

Import Process

The Swift compiler will look at the header files, compile them into Objective-C modules, and import them as native Swift APIs. The import process determines how the APIs (functions, classes, methods, and types) declared in Objective-C appear in Swift. This process will remap:

- Objective-C types to equivalent Swift types.
- Certain Objective-C types to Swift native types, such as `NSArray` to `Array`, or `NSString` to `String`.
- Certain Objective-C concepts to equivalent Swift concepts.

> **Note** You cannot import C++ code directly into Swift, you have to export your code wrapped in an Objective-C interface.

The process of importing Swift code into Objective-C works similarly.

Interoperability

What happens when you import Objective-C code into Swift? First, pointers are mapped to Swift optionals or regular objects depending on how you expose the API marked with nullability macros as described in the next section.

```
NSString *myString = nil
```

will be imported as:

```
var myString : NSString? = nil
```

Actually, that's not strictly true. The second thing that happens is that certain types, such as `NSString`, are mapped to native Swift objects such as `String`, so the actual mapping is:

```
var myString : String? = nil
```

The Objective-C type `id` is mapped to the Swift `AnyObject` protocol. This protocol can represent an instance of any object type derived from NSObject, just as id represents any object in Objective-C.

```
id myObject = nil;
var myObject : AnyObject? = nil
var myObject1 : AnyObject = NSString()
```

> **Note** The `AnyObject` protocol represents a safe object. If you'd like to be able to assign a nil value, it has to be boxed in an optional.

Keep in mind that, in Swift, once a variable is assigned a type, you cannot change the type of that variable. AnyObject is different, however. It can hold different types of Objective-C objects.

```
var myObject : AnyObject = NSString()
myObject = NSArray()
```

Since AnyObject does not represent a specific type, you are allowed to call any Objective-C method or access any property without having to cast the type to a specific class.

```
let myObject : AnyObject = UIView(frame: CGRectZero)
let myView = UIView()
myObject.addSubview(myView)
```

The types of objects are determined at runtime in Objective-C, and that's also true for AnyObject: its type is determined at runtime. Because of this, it's possible to write unsafe code. If you try to call a method or access a property that doesn't exist for a type, this will cause a runtime error similar to Objective-C. Let's say you try to call a method from NSArray, such as objectAtIndex(0):

```
let myObject : AnyObject = UIView(frame: CGRectZero)
let myValue = myObject.objectAtIndex(0)
```

There's no syntax error, but you'll get an error at runtime because the method objectAtIndex doesn't exist for UIView. If you run this program, you'll get a runtime error and crash the program. The error message will say, "unrecognized selector sent to instance," which is an Objective-C runtime telling you that the method you're trying to call on an object doesn't exist.

You can work around this problem by using optionals. What's really happening in the preceding code is something like this:

```
myObject.objectAtIndex!(0)
```

Notice the implicit unwrapping operation. You can rewrite that code with an optional:

```
let myValue : AnyObject? = myObject.objectAtIndex?(0)
```

Now the code won't cause the runtime error and crash the program when the objectAtIndex is called, because this method does not exist. The runtime will check the availability of the method and set the value of myValue to nil.

A method call on AnyObject may or may not succeed at runtime; that value returned from the method call is returned as an optional AnyObject? type. This object represents AnyObject before you can use it; you will have to cast it to the type of object you are expecting and then unbox it.

Let's say the call succeeds and you get some instance of an object. You should check the type:

```
if let myImage = myValue as? UIImage {
    // do something with image
}
```

Here we are checking if the instance returned from the method call is of type UIImage. If that's true, we assign unbox it to myImage and then we can safely use it in our code.

Nullability and Optionals

Objective-C uses raw pointer to represent objects and they can become nil, but in Swift every valid object is guaranteed to have a valid value, and if the object cannot have a valid value then it is wrapped in an optional. You have seen this from the previous examples that all Objective-C objects by default will be imported as optionals even if you know they will never be nil.

The latest release of Objective-C has solved this problem by allowing you to add nullability annotations to properties, parameters, and return values to let Swift import process know which objects can be nil.

Individual object types can add the keywords `_Nullable` or `_Nonnull` depending if they can be `null` or not: the _Nullable tells the compiler that this pointer is allowed to have a NULL o nil value. And _Nonnull tells the compiler that the pointer must have a valid value at all times. If you try to assign a nil value to _Nonnull type the compiler will not compile you code. These keywords must be added after the pointer symbol.

```
- (TheObject * _Nullable)itemWithName:(NSString * _Nonnull)name
{
   return [[TheObject alloc] init];
}
- (TheObject * _Nullable)itemWithName:(NSString * _Nonnull)name
{
   return nil;
}
```

This code tells the compiler that this method can return a null value but must not be initialized with null value; the argument name must have a valid string.

You can use these keywords almost anywhere you can use the const keyword in C. You have to remember that there is an underscore at the beginning and you have to capitalize the first letter. Well for most common/simple cases there is a better way.

```
- (nullable TheObject *)anotherItemWithName:(nonnull NSString *)name;
```

Much better, you put the keyword before the type declaration.

You use the same keywords for properties either using the basic or prettier versions.

```
@property(strong, nonnull, nonatomic) NSString *name;
@property(strong, nonatomic) NSString * _Nullable anotherName;
```

You can also mark whole regions of files with nullability annotations using macro:

NS_ASSUME_NONNULL_BEGIN and NS_ASSUME_NONNULL_END: declarations between the beginning and end will be marked as nonnull.

Also keep in mind that once you explicitly mark any item with nullability annotation in a file, every item must be explicitly marked with nullability annotation. It's everything or none.

Now that you have updated your code with nullability, how does it appear in Swift?

Let's take a look at what it looks like before nullability annotations:

```
var name : String?
var anotherName : String?
func itemWithName(name : String!) -> TheObject?
```

Too many optionals, even if they cannot be null, after annotations:

```
var name : String
var anotherName: String?
func itemWithName(name : String) -> TheObject?
```

Object Initialization

Swift will import the init methods from Objective-C with the new Swift syntax; the regular - (instancetype)init will be imported as init(). If you have been a good Objective-C citizen and named your init methods that take arguments with initWithSomething:(Type *)type, those methods will be imported with following transformations:

- The methods will be named init.
- The string With will be dropped.
- In the remaining string (<Something>), the first letter will be lowercased and that string will become the name of the first argument.
- Any other arguments that exist will be added.

Here's what a fictional example looks like:

```
init(something : Type)
```

Let's take a look at a concrete example.

```
- (instancetype)initWithNibName:(NSString *)nibNameOrNil bundle:(NSBundle *)nibBundleOrNil;
```

will be mapped to

```
init(nibName nibNameOrNil: String?, bundle nibBundleOrNil: NSBundle?)
```

When creating an object, you don't need to call an alloc method that's done implicitly for you:

```
UIViewController *controller = [[UIViewController alloc] initWithNibName:nil bundle:nil];
```

```
let viewController = UIViewController(nibName: nil, bundle: nil)
```

Notice that we do not explicitly call the `init` method. `UIViewController.init(...)` is a syntax error; Swift will match the correct `init` method based in the arguments.

Factory methods for a type are also brought over with the same syntax as convenience `init` methods:

```
UIColor *color = [UIColor colorWithWhite:1.0f alpha:0.5f];
let color = UIColor(white: 1.0, alpha: 0.5)
```

Failable Initializers

In Objective-C, initializers explicitly return the object that was created. If the object creation fails, the initializer returns nil to tell the calling code that it has failed. In Swift, this pattern is called *failable initializers*. You name the failable initializer with an optional, so your init method name becomes `init?(...)`, which tells the compiler that this `init` method may fail and will return a `nil` if it does.

```
NSArray *array = [NSArray arrayWithContentsOfFile:@"/tmp/myArray.plist"];
```

This call to create an array from a file can fail. It might fail if the file doesn't exist or if it cannot be parsed into an array. The initializer will be imported as

```
convenience init?(contentsOfFile path: String)
```

The only time you return explicitly from an init method is if you are returning nil. In this example we try to read the data from the file path that was given; if the contents were not able to be read, we fail and return.

```
class MyObject {
    init?(path : String) {
        guard let values = NSArray(contentsOfFile: path) else {
            return nil
        }
        // Do somthing with values
    }
}
```

Properties

To access Objective-C properties in Swift, you use the familiar dot syntax:

```
let view = UIView(frame: CGRectZero)
view.hidden = false
view.backgroundColor = UIColor.whiteColor()
```

We accessed two properties of view: one takes a simple Boolean value and the other takes a UIColor instance.

One thing to notice is that `whiteColor` is not a property. Because it has parentheses, it's a function. In Objective-C, properties are a user-level interface; the compiler generates methods, so when you are accessing properties you are actually calling methods without any arguments. Why is this distinction important? Because Swift will only import properties from Objective-C as properties if they are declared using the `@property` syntax; otherwise they will be imported as methods.

Methods

As you've seen in previous chapters, to call methods in Swift you use the dot syntax similar to properties. When importing methods into Swift, they get mapped to the Swift method syntax:

- The Swift function name derives from the first part of the Objective-C method name.
- The first argument is mapped as an unnamed argument.
- The rest of the arguments are mapped with names.

For example,

```
[collectionView dequeueReusableCellWithReuseIdentifier:CellIdentifier
forIndexPath:indexPath];
```

will become

```
collectionView.dequeueReusableCellWithReuseIdentifier(CellIdentifier, forIndexPath:
indexPath)
```

Also the internal and external argument names will be added correctly. Let's take a look at an example that you have probably used previously. The second argument has both the external argument name cellForItemAtIndexPath, and the internal name indexPath.

```
func collectionView(collectionView: UICollectionView, cellForItemAtIndexPath indexPath:
NSIndexPath) -> UICollectionViewCell {
```

Blocks

Objective-C blocks are imported as closures. In Objective-C you define a block variable using the syntax:

```
void (^myBlockVariable)(BOOL finished, NSString *result) = ^(BOOL finished, NSString
*result) {
// Block implementation
}
```

This block is named myBlockVariable. It takes two arguments and returns no results. In Swift, it would look like this:

```
let myBlockVariable : (Bool, String) -> Void = {(finished, result) in
// Block implementation
}
```

The syntax may look different but they are compatible, which means when a method is expecting a block as an argument, you can pass a closure as a value. There are some differences, however.

Since Swift functions are named closures, you can pass a function in place of a closure as long as the types match, meaning the argument list and return type are the same.

Closures capture variables the same way as blocks but with one difference. In Objective-C blocks, the variables are copied and are immutable. In Swift, they are mutable and you use the __block keyword for the captured variables.

Object Comparison

When comparing objects, you can compare two properties. The first type of comparison is if two objects are pointing to the same instance of a type:

```
NSObject *myObject = [[NSObject alloc] init];
NSObject *anotherObject = myObject;
```

Both of these objects point to the exact same instance of NSObject. In Objective-C you compare two objects using the isEqual: method from the NSObject.

```
BOOL equal = [myObject isEqual:anotherObject];
```

In Swift you use the identity operator, === (three equal signs).

The other type of comparison is where two objects point to two different objects but have the same contents:

```
NSString *myString = @"My String";
NSString *anotherString = @"My String";
```

Even though they have the same content, and despite the fact they point to two different objects, this is called equality. In Objective-C you use the isEqualToString: method to compare if two strings are the same. In Swift you use the equal to operator, == (two equal signs), to determine whether the contents of the objects are same.

If you derive a Swift class from an NSObject, Swift will implement the == operator and call the isEqual: method. So you should implement this method in your Swift subclasses. If you don't derive a Swift class from NSObject and you try to use the isEqual: method in Objective-C, you'll get a runtime error so make sure to implement the isEqual: method.

Type Compatibility

Objective-C uses a dynamic runtime while Swift uses both dynamic and static runtimes, depending on how the type is defined. If the type is derived from:

An Objective-C class, then Swift uses a dynamic runtime. Otherwise, it doesn't use a dynamic runtime unless you specifically tell it that a dynamic runtime is needed.

When importing Objective-C into Swift, you don't have to do anything specific. You have access to all the properties, methods, and so on.

When exposing Swift classes to Objective-C, you can control how they are exposed. In Swift you can have classes that inherit from Objective-C-based classes such as NSObject, or those that are purely Swift classes.

If you inherit a Swift class from an Objective-C class, all of its properties, methods, subscripts, and initializers become available to other Objective-C classes.

If you have a class that doesn't inherit from Objective-C, You cannot export to Objective-C:

If you use the other keywords, such as `@IBOutlet`, `@IBAction`, and `@NSManaged`, the `@objc` attribute is automatically added.

When exporting Swift methods to Objective-C, the compiler will map the method names correctly to their Objective-C equivalents:

```
func myFunction(argument1 : ArgumentType) -> ReturnType
```

This method will be translated to

```
- (ReturnType)myFunction:(ArgumentType *)argument1
```

The exception to this rule is the initializer method. By default, `initWith` is added to the beginning of the name `init`. So `(myArgument : ArgumentType)` will be translated to `- (instancetype)initWithMyArgument:(ArgumentType *)myArgument`.

Remember that Swift can use the full set of UNICODE characters for its names, including class name, methods, properties, and so forth. Also, Swift uses namespaces and prepends the module name to the class names. If you have a class called `MyClass` in your application named `MyApplication` (which is a module), the full name of the class would be `MyApplication.MyClass`. To work around these issues, the `@objc` attribute has an extended form where you specify the Objective-C names. In Swift you can have a class named 🐶🐮, but in Objective-C, if you try to name the class using non-ASCII characters, it would cause a compile-time error. You can give an explicit Objective-C name to your class using `@objc(DogCow)`. If you do not give an Objective-C name to a Swift class that uses non-ASCII characters, that class will not be exported to the Objective-C runtime. Explicitly giving an Objective-C name also removes the namespaces.

```
@objc(DogCow)
public class 🐶🐮 {
}
```

Even if the name of your class is not in non-ASCII characters but you just want to remove the namespaces, you need to do this:

```
@objc(DogCow)
public class DogCow {
}
```

You can also do the same with method names. For example, func ∑ (array : [Double]) -> Double needs to be rewritten so Objective-C can correctly use the method:

```
@objc(sum:)
func Σ(array : [Double]) -> Double
```

Objective-C Generics

Apple has added what it calls lightweight generics to make interoperability with Swift easier. Let's say you are working with some strings and you need to store them in an array, your typical code would look like this:

```
NSMutableArray *stringsArray = [[NSMutableArray alloc] init];
[stringsArray addObject:@"My String1"];
[stringsArray addObject:@"My String2"];
[stringsArray addObject:[[NSArray alloc] init]];
```

But as you know, NSMutableArray will hold any valid object type, so when you get values returned you may not get a NSString as with the third item; it's an array and if you try to use any string methods your program will crash, or if it is a string you have to cast it, because the return type of objectAtIndex is id.

```
NSString *result = (NSString *)[stringsArray objectAtIndex:0];
```

With generics you can tell NSArray what kind of object the array can hold.

```
NSMutableArray<NSString *>*stringsArray = [[NSMutableArray alloc] init];
[stringsArray addObject:@"My String1"];
[stringsArray addObject:@"My String2"];
[stringsArray addObject:[[NSArray alloc] init]];
```

We tell the compiler that we only want to hold NSString type; now we get a warning when adding the last item. Also when getting the value you don't have to cast.

```
NSMutableArray<NSString *>*stringsArray = [[NSMutableArray alloc] init];
[stringsArray addObject:@"My String1"];
[stringsArray addObject:@"My String2"];

NSString *result = [stringsArray objectAtIndex:0];
```

This works the same way with NSDictionary: you can define, and you give the key type and value type.

```
NSMutableDictionary<NSNumber *, NSString *> *dictionary = [[NSMutableDictionary alloc] init];
```

You can also create Objective-C with generics by giving generic names:

```
@interface TheObject<T> : NSObject
@property(strong, nonnull, nonatomic) T name;
@property(strong, nonatomic) T _Nullable anotherName;

- (TheObject * _Nullable)itemWithName:(T _Nonnull)name;
- (nullable TheObject *)anotherItemWithName:(nonnull T)name;
```

Now you can use a specific type to create new instance:

```
TheObject<NSString *> *myObject = [[TheObject alloc] init];
```

Once you do that then Swift can import these in a type-safe manner. In our strings array example, without generics it will look like this:

```
let  stringsArray = [AnyObject]()
```

with lightweight generics:

```
let stringsArray = [String]()
```

> **Note** This is purely a compiler level change: the runtime ABI has not changed, so your code will be backward compatible.

Dynamic Dispatch

Even after adding the `@objc` attribute to your methods, there's still no guarantee of using dynamic dispatch. The compiler can optimize the code at will for performance and skip the dynamic dispatch. Typically, you don't need to worry about this, but sometimes you need to have that certainty that the method or property will be called using the dynamic dispatch system.

You use the keyword `dynamic` to force the dynamic dispatch, usually in the case of key-value-observation (KVO), or if you want to switch method implementations at runtime:

```
dynamic public func myFunction() -> Void
```

Selectors

In Objective-C you can create a selector object (SEL) using the @selector(nameOfSelector) that can be assigned as an action. The SEL object is imported to Swift as a Selector type.

```
SEL mySelector = @selector(mySelector:);
var mySelector  : Selector = "mySelector:"
```

You will notice that we just assigned a string literal to the selector type, because a string literal can be converted to a Selector type. So you don't have to explicitly create a Selector object; you can just use a string literal where a selector is required as an argument.

```
let barButtonItem = UIBarButtonItem(barButtonSystemItem: .Done, target: self, action: "done:")
```

> **Note** The performSelector class of methods is not imported into Swift because of safety reasons.

Property Attributes

Some of the attributes that were used when defining properties will be used and others will be discarded. The default behavior for a property in Swift is strong. In Objective-C it's assigned; weak has the same meaning in both Swift and Objective-C. There are no read-write or read-only attributes. You define those by using either the let and var keywords or by providing either getter only or getter and setter.

The copy attribute is translated to the @NSCopying protocol so the type must conform to that protocol. There is no @dynamic keyword needed. This was a key requirement for Core Data objects; for that, the @NSManaged keyword is provided.

Namespaces and Class

I've already talked about namespaces and how the names of Swift classes have module names prepended to them. One solution is to export them using the @objc(name) to give an Objective-C compatible name.

If you don't want to do that, you can use the fully qualified names when using those classes. If the class is in a framework called MySuperFramework, you'd use the class name MySuperFramework.ClassName. Even if you don't have a framework, your application is a namespace. If the application name is MyApplication, the fully qualified name is MyApplication.ClassName. Any time you have to use a string for a name, such as NSClassFromString, you'll need to provide a fully qualified name:

```
Class class = NSClassFromString(@"MyApplication.ClassName")
```

When you work with Core Data objects, the interface expects names without namespaces. In the editor, where you specify the name of the class for an entity, you need to provide fully qualified names.

Cocoa Data Types

Swift will automatically map some of the foundation types to native Swift types, as shown in Table 20-1.

Table 20-1. *Swift foundation types mapped to native Swift types*

Foundation Types	Swift Types
NSString, NSMutableString	String
NSArray, NSMutableArray	[AnyObject], Array<AnyObject>
NSDictionary, NSMutableDictionary	[NSObject : AnyObject]. Dictionary<NSObject, AnyObject>
NSNumber	Int, UInt. ...

Foundation Functions

Most of the Foundation functions will be imported into Swift, such as `NSLog`. On the other hand, `NSAssert` functions do not carry over. Use the native `assert` function instead.

Core Foundation

Core Foundation data types are automatically imported as Swift classes. For any Core Foundation functions that provide memory annotation, such as `CF_RETURNS_RETAINED` or `CF_RETURNS_NOT_RETAINED`, the memory is automatically managed. You don't have to call the `CFRetain`, `CFRelease`, or `CFAutorelease` functions, even when you create those objects.

When Swift imports Core Foundation types, the names get changed and the `Ref` suffix is dropped. For example, `CFArrayRef` will be imported as `CFArray`. One exception: `CFTypeRef` is completely mapped to `AnyObject`. Anywhere you use `CFTypeRef` you can now use `AnyObject`.

With any functions that are annotated with memory management where the compiler can't automatically manage the memory for those Core Foundation types, they are returned wrapped in the `Unmanaged<T>` structure. In that case you have to use a couple of functions to unwrap those to objects whose memory can be managed. These functions will convert an unmanaged object to a managed object.

- `takeUnretainedValue`: This function will return the wrapped object as unretained.
- `takeRetainedValue`: This function will return the wrapped object as retained.

In the following function, I haven't defined how the memory is managed:

```
CFStringRef MyStringManipulationFunction(CFStringRef string)
```

This function will be imported as:

```
func MyStringManipulationFunction(string : CFString!)  -> Unmanaged<CFString>!
```

To unbox and have Swift manage the memory, I use:

```
var myResult = MyStringManipulationFunction(string).takeUnretainedValue()
```

Interacting with C

Objective-C is a superset of C, which means everything that C provides is also brought into Swift because it is part of Objective-C. The C primitive types are mapped as shown in Table 20-2.

Table 20-2. C primitive types mapped

C Type	Swift Type
int, short, long	CInt, CShort, CLong
Bool	CBool
unsigned int , unsigned short, unsigned long	CUnsignedInt, CUnsignedShort, CUnsignedLong
char, signed char	CChar
unsigned char	CUnsignedChar
float, double	CFloat, CDouble
wchar_t , char16_t, char32_t	CWideChar, CChar16, CChar32

Even though Swift will import these data types, it's recommended you use Swift native equivalent types.

Keep in mind as well that global constants are imported as Swift constants and simple macros are imported as Swift constants. For example, `#define MY_PI 3.14` will be imported as `let MY_PI = 3.14`. Complex macros are not brought over.

Summary

Even though Swift is a new language with a new syntax and runtime, it still works with the existing Objective-C API. There are pain points because Swift is trying to do Objective-C without the bad parts; and, for some time, we'll still have to deal with the existing code base. Pay close attention to the translation layer and to how the two-way bridge works. For now, it's recommended that you be verbose as to how you'd like to exchange APIs between Objective-C and Swift.

Chapter 21

Working with Core Data

Core Data is a framework that allows you to maintain an ordered data store for either in-memory or permanent storage. It is akin to a database, but it's not a database in a traditional sense, it's not a relational database management system (RDBMS). Core Data can use a traditional database as a lower layer for external storage; SQLite is one of the storage mechanisms it supports.

Core Data is an object graph and persistence store framework that provides a high-level data model via entities and the relationships among those entities. It also provides fetch requests to retrieve data that meets certain criteria. Developers use Xcode's entity editor to define the object models and relationships.

Core Data is a small framework with only few classes, but it provides quite a bit of functionality, and it takes some getting used to. Some of its features include:

- Support for key value observation (KVO) and key value coding (KVC)
- Schema migration
- Relationship maintenance
- Undo support
- Change propagation
- Filtering
- Complex queries

Here's the basic life cycle of the Core Data stack:

- Set up the stack.
- Modify the objects if needed.
- Save the objects if needed.
- Tear down the stack.

Now that you have some idea of what Core Data can do, let's take a look at the classes provided by the framework and how they fit in the life cycle of the application.

NSManagedObjectContext

`NSManagedObjectContext` is a temporary area where the existing objects from a backing store get brought in and modified, or where you can create new objects. If you don't save the context explicitly, these changes are not saved between the application restarts. You can think of this as a scratch pad. (On iOS this means explicitly killing an app, not just going to background mode).

NSManagedObject

Any object (entity) you define that needs to work with the Core Data stack must be a subclass of `NSManagedObject`. These objects live in the context until they are saved to the backing store.

NSManagedObjectModel

`NSManagedObjectModel` defines the schema for your entities. This is where you specify the properties of your entities and the kinds of relationships they will have with other entities. The combination of entities and relationships is the object graph. You'll be interfacing with an instance of this object.

NSPersistentStoreCoordinator

`NSPersistentStoreCoordinator` is the go-between for the backing store (memory or disk) and the `ManagedObjectContext`. When you need to load or save objects from the store, this object will do that for you.

NSFetchRequest

`NSFetchRequest` lets you define how you'd like to load your data from the store. You can define criteria such as the entity name (one of subclass of `NSManagedObject`); the sort order (how you want your objects sorted, if at all); and a predicate (how to match the objects you want).

NSPredicate

`NSPredicate` defines how to match objects when searching for them in external storage. This could be the name of a person, for example, and it's evaluated against each object that's read. If it evaluates to true, the object is loaded.

Creating An Application

With some background on how Core Data works in hand, it's time to start building an an iOS application. Start Xcode if it's not already started. To create a new project, select iOS ➤ Application ➤ Master-Detail Application (Figure 21-1) and call it Car Collection (Figure 21-2). Make sure to select the Use Core Data option in the project creation workflow.

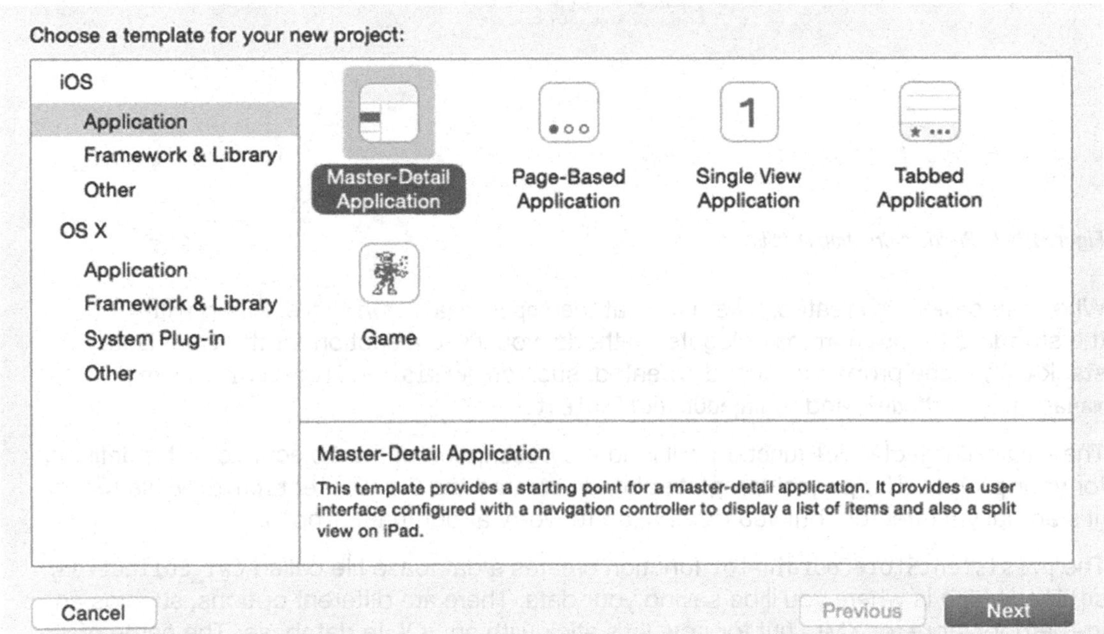

Figure 21-1. Application Template

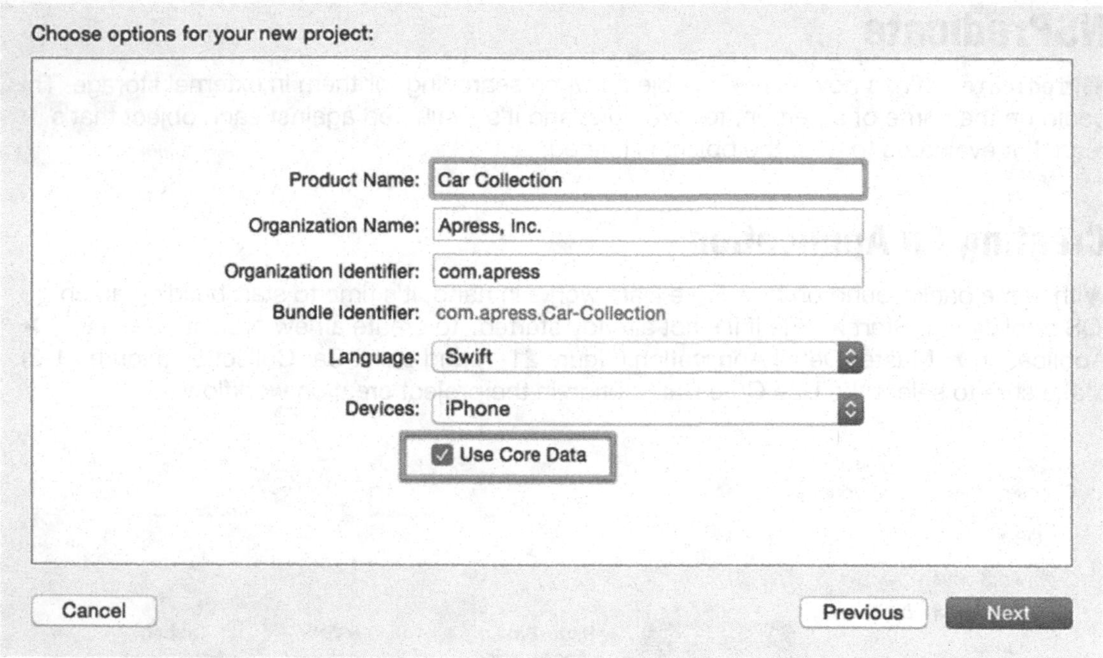

Figure 21-2. Projects Creation Details

When the project is created, take a look at the `AppDelegate.swift` file. Along with the standard `UIApplication` delegate methods, you'll see a section for the Core Data stack with some properties already created, such as `persistentStoreCoordinator`, `managedObjectModel`, and `managedObjectContext`.

The `managedObjectModel` function will load the description of the objects you'll be defining for your project. The project template already created the `Car_Collection.momd` file for you (it's actually a directory but you don't need to worry about that for now).

The `persistentStoreCoordinator` function creates a database file called `Car_Collection.sqlite`, which is where you'll be saving your data. There are different options, such as an in-memory store, or XML, but for now let's stick with an SQLite database. The name of the file is based on the template but you can change it if you like. One of the items that's required is the `ManagedObjectModel` instance. This allows the `persistantStoreCoordinator` to correctly story entities the backing store.

And, finally, the `managedObjectContext` is where you'll be adding new objects and saving to the database.

Defining Data Objects

One of the other files is `Car_Collection.xcdatamodeld`, which is where you define the properties and entities you'll be using (Figure 21-3). Select the data model file. In the editor, you'll see types of objects, such as entities and fetch requests, on the left. Once you select an entity, you have the object type-specific editor. Entities include:

- Attributes, such as name or height of a person.
- Relationships to other entities; there are many types of relationships:
  - One-to-one, where an object references one other object; for example, one person having one spouse.
  - One-to-many, where an object references many other objects; for example, one parent having many children.
  - Many-to-many, where any number of objects can reference many other objects, and the reverse; for example, siblings having other siblings.
- Fetched properties, which are similar to relationships, but with these differences:
  - Values are calculated using a fetch request.
  - Fetched properties can be ordered, so they are stored in arrays instead of sets.
  - Fetched properties are evaluated lazily and the results are cached.

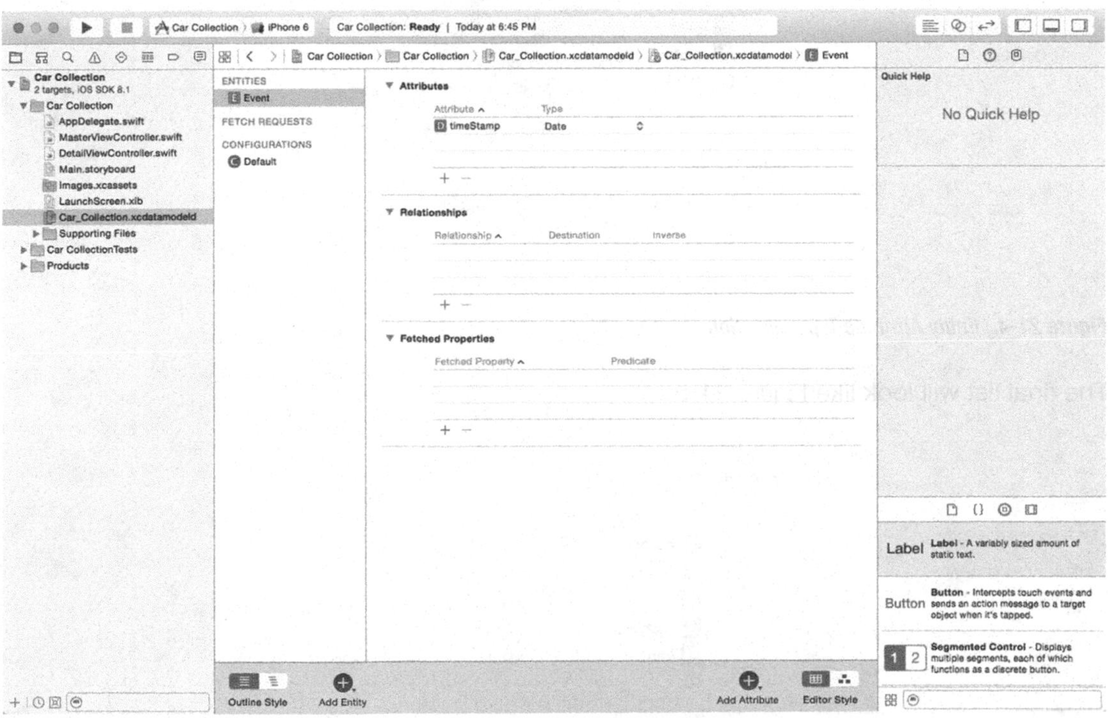

Figure 21-3. CoreData Entities Editor

There's a default entity called Event that you don't really need, so delete it. Now let's create the `Car` entity and add some attributes to it. Select the Add Entity button on the bottom of the editor. A new entity named `Entity` will be added to the entity list. Rename that to Car and add the attributes listed in Table 21-1.

Table 21-1. Attributes to be added to new entity

Attribute Name	Attribute Type
make	String
model	String
year	Date
color	String
doors	Integer 16

Under the Attributes section, select the + button to add new attributes. After adding each attribute, set its name and the type. You select the type by choosing from the pop-up menu (Figure 21-4).

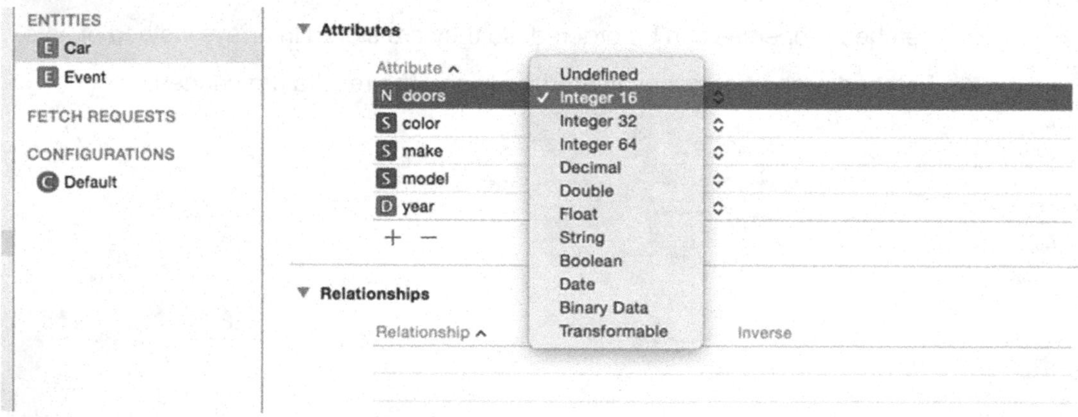

Figure 21-4. Entity Attribute Type Selection

The final list will look like Figure 21-5.

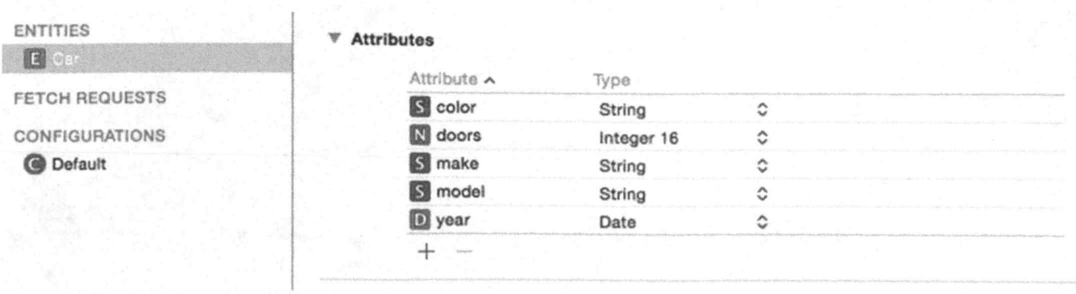

Figure 21-5. Car Entity Attributes

If you'd like to add more properties, you can do that whenever you like. We are going to work with these for now.

The next step is to tell the controller what kind of objects to load and show. From the project navigator, look at the MasterViewController.swift file. Most of the code in this file is boilerplate that's needed by the `tableView` to show the objects. You will be modifying the `NSFetchResultsController`, the object that creates the fetch request and asks the `managedObjectContext` to load the objects based on the criteria you've set.

Look for the implementation for variable fetchedResultsController, specifically the NSEntityDescription which tells the fetchedController what kind of entity to look for. Currently it is looking for the default entity, you need to rename the entity currently called "`Event`". Change that to `Car`, and the line will look like this:

```
let entity = NSEntityDescription.entityForName("Car", inManagedObjectContext:
self.managedObjectContext!)
```

The next line to modify is the NSSortDescriptor key, which is the sort descriptor. This is where you tell how to sort the objects for displaying. Currently the sort is dependent on the `timeStamp` attribute, but you don't have to use that. In this case you should sort by the name of the car, so change it to use the `model` attribute:

```
let sortDescriptor = NSSortDescriptor(key: "model", ascending: false)
```

Now that fetching is corrected, let's correct the configuration of the cell. The implementation displays the `timeStamp` attribute, so let's change that as well. In the function `configureCell`, change it to use `model`

```
cell.textLabel!.text = object.valueForKey("model") as? String
```

The reason you need to cast this as `String` is that `valueForKey` will return an object of `AnyObject` (or in Objective-C, `id`) and the label only takes a String type. And you know that model is of string type, so you can just cast it.

If you build and run now, you'll see nothing but an empty list, with edit and add buttons. That's good. What we did was create the car collection database on external storage and load the empty data set, with correct layout for our Car entity.

The next thing to do is add a new object. Select the add button. Oops! That crashed the application! Let's look at the reason. Here's the error message:

```
2015-02-07 20:26:54.924 Car Collection[16383:2800553] *** Terminating app due to
uncaught exception 'NSUnknownKeyException', reason: '[<NSManagedObject 0x7f9033a0d570>
setValue:forUndefinedKey:]: the entity Car is not key value coding-compliant for the key
"timeStamp".'
```

This indicates that you tried to add a new `Car` and to set the `timeStamp` attribute, but `Car` doesn't have that attribute. Go back to the MasterViewController.swift file and look at the `insertNewObject` function. It's a simple method that creates a new object in the context and adds the `timeStamp` of when it was created. However, the `Car` object needs more attributes, so you'll have to create a new view to edit the properties.

Adding an Object Editor

Go to the Main.storyboard file to add a new view controller that will let you edit the attributes for your `Car`. Start by adding a new view controller to the project by selecting File ➤ New ➤ File... and selecting Cocoa Touch Class (Figure 21-6).

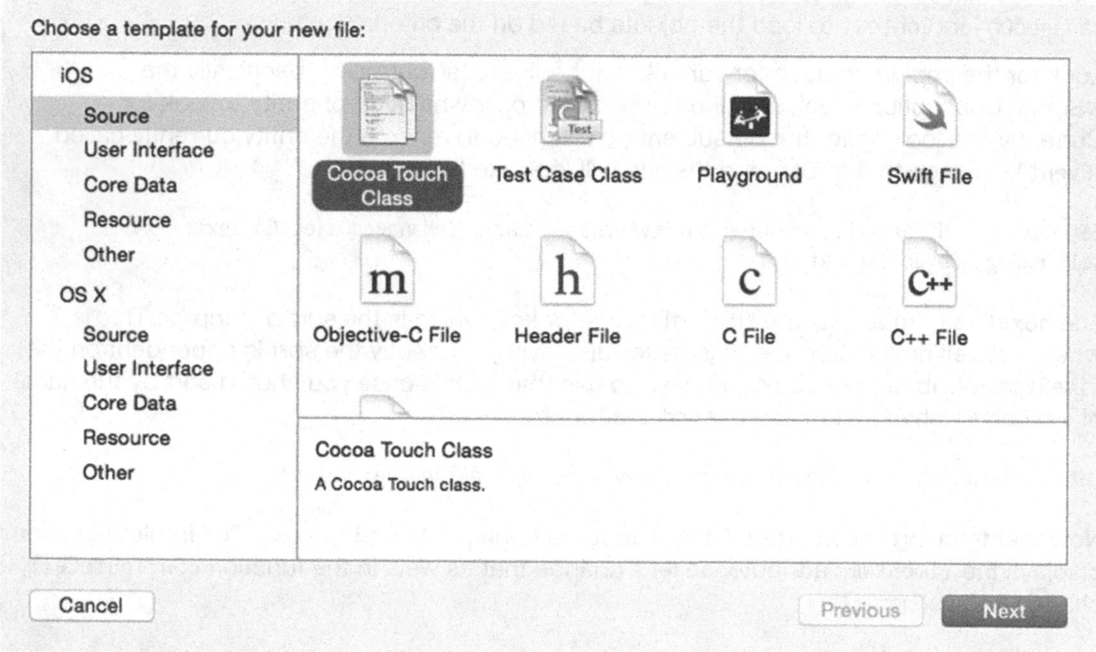

Figure 21-6. Creating new Controller

Then name the new controller as shown in Figure 21-7.

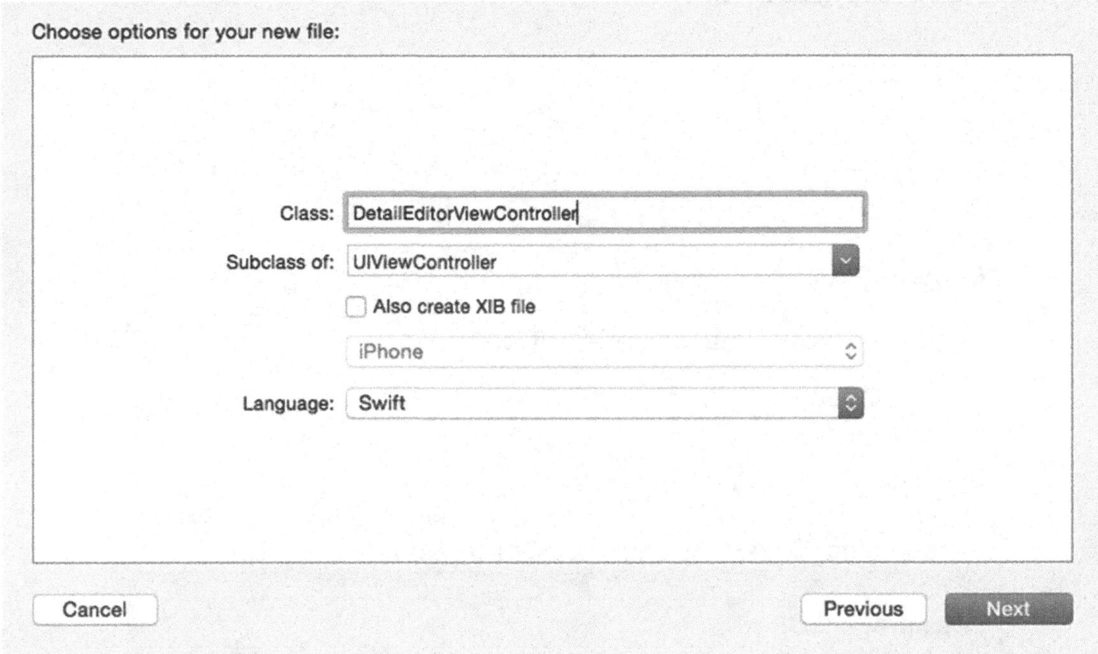

***Figure 21-7.** Naming the New Controller*

Select the View Controller object from the object palette (Figure 21-8) and drag it to the storyboard.

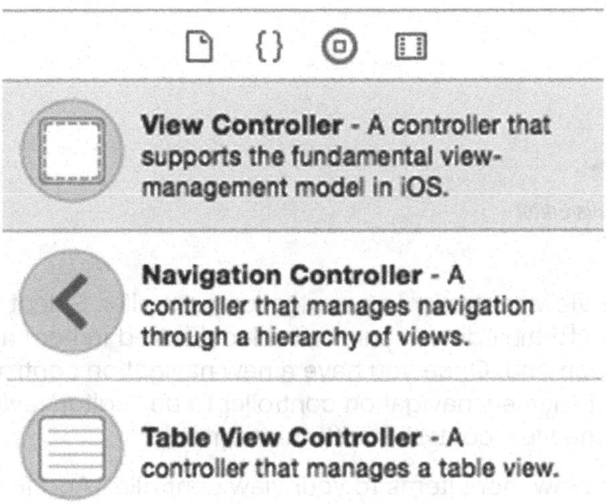

***Figure 21-8.** Object Template Pane*

When you have the controller in the storyboard, select the view controller and then select the identity inspector. Then change the custom class to the new view controller, and add the storyboard identifier (Figure 21-9).

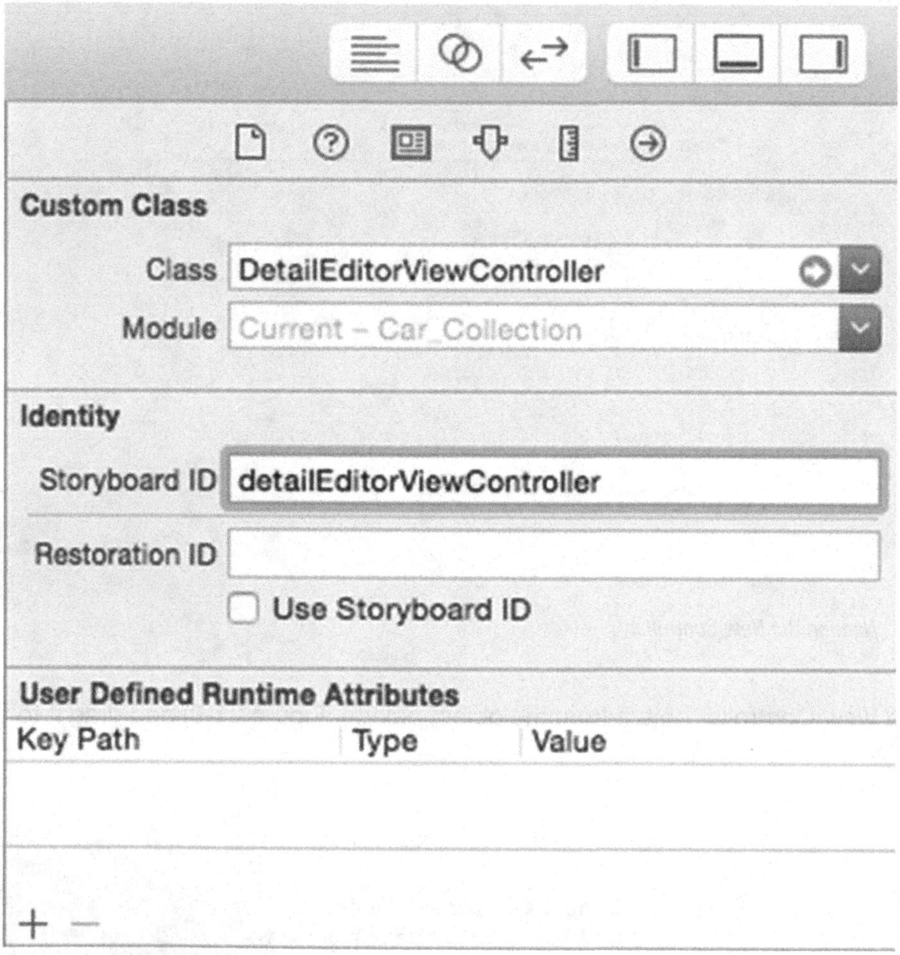

Figure 21-9. *Controller Details Editor*

Now you'll embed this view controller in a navigation controller. Select the view controller in the storyboard, then go to the editor menu and select Embed In Item and then Navigation Controller under the submenu. Once you have a new navigation controller, set the storyboard identifier for the new navigation controller to be "editorNavigationController". You'll be instantiating the view controller with this name.

Now you need to add a few more items to your view controller. Add four text fields, Make, Model, Color, and Doors and set the placeholder for the text fields in order to prompt the user to enter those values (Figure 21-10).

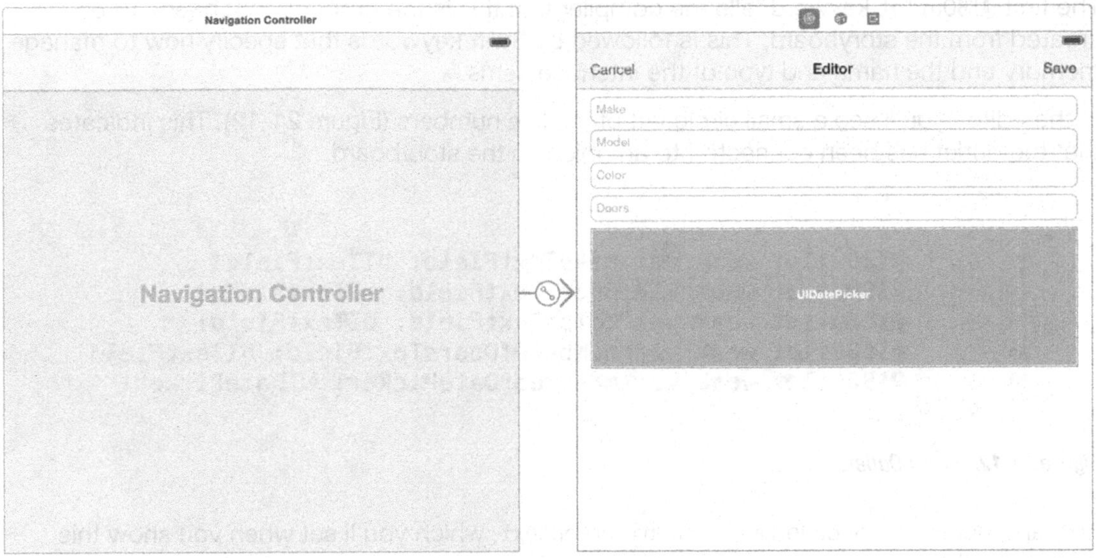

Figure 21-10. Editor Controller with Navigation Controller

Then add a date-picker object where you can set the year for the car. Also add Save and Cancel buttons so you can either save or dismiss the view controller depending on whether you want to save or cancel the new Car.

Next you need to add code to populate the view with your data if you have an existing object, or you need to create a new one. Connect each of these items to your controller outlets. Select the view controller and open the assistant editor.

Select each item and then press the control key and drag to the source file (this is called control-drag). This will create outlets for each item. You should now have five outlets with appropriate names.

Once you control-drag to your source file, the editor will ask you to name each outlet. The editor will prefill most of the defaults for the outlet that make sense. All you have to do is enter the name of the outlet (Figure 21-11).

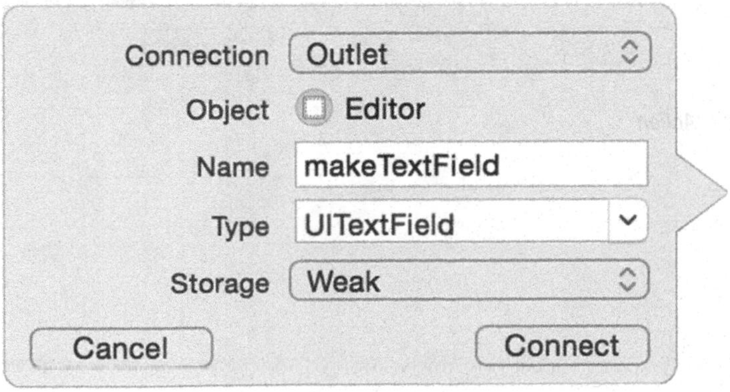

Figure 21-11. Adding Outlet

The first @IBOutlet keyword tells the compiler that this is the property that needs to be created from the storyboard. This is followed by Swift keywords that specify how to manage memory and the name and type of the interface items.

In the editor, you'll see a small circle left of the line numbers (Figure 21-12). This indicates that the outlet has been connected to an object in the storyboard.

```
@IBOutlet weak var makeTextField: UITextField!
@IBOutlet weak var modelTextField: UITextField!
@IBOutlet weak var colorTextField: UITextField!
@IBOutlet weak var numberOfDoorsTextField: UITextField!
@IBOutlet weak var makeYearDatePicker: UIDatePicker!
```

Figure 21-12. Editor Outlets

Add another property called managedObjectContext, which you'll set when you show this view controller.

```
var managedObjectContext: NSManagedObjectContext? = nil
```

Make sure to add the import Core Data statement at the top of the file. This will ensure you have the Core Data module available in this file.

Now you need to connect the Save and Cancel buttons so they can perform some actions for you. This time when you control-drag the Cancel button, you need to change the type of connection in the pop-up to Action instead of Outlet, and make the name "cancel" (Figure 21-13).

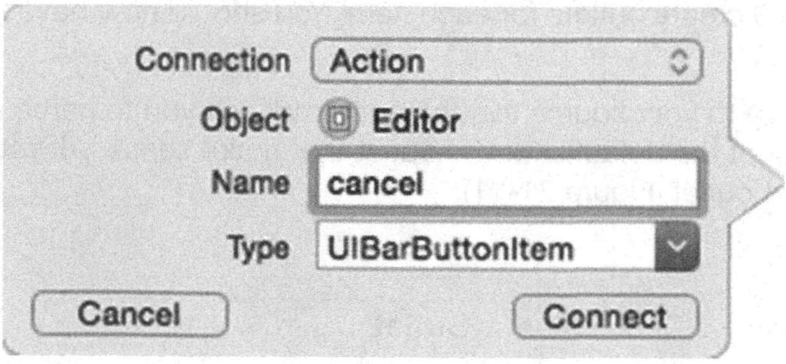

Figure 21-13. Adding an Action

And after setting the attributes and selecting Connect, the editor will add an action function that will be called when you select the Cancel button. The function is just like other instance functions except with the `@IBAction` keyword before the `func` keyword to let the compiler know that this function will be called from an object in the storyboard.

```
@IBAction func cancel(sender: UIBarButtonItem) {
}
```

This is an empty function so add some code to dismiss the view controller:

```
@IBAction func cancel(sender: UIBarButtonItem) {
self.presentingViewController?.dismissViewControllerAnimated(true, completion: nil)
}
```

Now do the same with the Save button. First, name the function save.

```
@IBAction func save(sender: UIBarButtonItem) {
}
```

Then fill in code for the save function:

```
@IBAction func save(sender: UIBarButtonItem) {
    let context = self.managedObjectContext
    let entityName = "Car"
    let newManagedObject = NSEntityDescription.insertNewObjectForEntityForName(entityName,
    inManagedObjectContext: context!) as NSManagedObject

    newManagedObject.setValue(self.makeTextField.text ?? "Unknown Make", forKey: "make")
    newManagedObject.setValue(self.modelTextField.text ?? "Unknown Model", forKey: "model")
    newManagedObject.setValue(self.colorTextField.text ?? "Unknown Color", forKey: "color")
    let doors : NSString = self.numberOfDoorsTextField.text ?? "2"
    let number = NSNumber(int: doors.intValue)
    newManagedObject.setValue(number, forKey: "doors")
    newManagedObject.setValue(self.makeYearDatePicker.date, forKey: "year")

    var error: NSError? = nil
    if !context!.save(&error) {
    }

    self.presentingViewController?.dismissViewControllerAnimated(true, completion: nil)
}
```

The first line creates a local reference to the context and the second sets the name of the entity to create.

The next line actually creates an entity of type `Car` and inserts it into the `managedObjectContext`. If you don't set any attributes, the entity would still exist. But let's add some.

The next three lines take the values from the text fields and add those to the new entity. The line after that is a bit tricky because you're setting the type of the doors to integer. You have to store the integer as an NSNumber because Core Data stores objects, not primitives. And, lastly, the code just takes the date and adds the year.

After setting the attributes, save your object to storage by calling the save instance method on the managedObjectContext.

Finally, dismiss the controller, and go back to the list of cars.

Showing the Editor

Now that you have an editor, how do you show it? Remember that you have an insertNewObject in the MasterViewController. You're going to remove the existing code and replace it with the following code to instantiate the navigation controller and present it.

```
func insertNewObject(sender: AnyObject) {
        let navController = self.storyboard?.
        instantiateViewControllerWithIdentifier("editorNavigationController") as?
        UINavigationController
        let editorViewController = navController?.topViewController as
        DetailEditorViewController
        editorViewController.managedObjectContext = self.managedObjectContext;
        self.navigationController?.presentViewController(navController!, animated: true,
        completion: nil);
}
```

This function will instantiate the navigation controller you added, along with its root view controller, which is the editor controller. Get your editor controller and then set the managedObjectContext since you want to create objects in this context, and then present it on the screen.

Now experiment with this and add some cars. Once you add a car and dismiss the editor by saving, you'll see that car immediately show up in your list.

Entity Classes

You probably noticed that you didn't actually create an entity class called Car and that we have used the setValue:forKey: method on NSManagedObject to set the attributes, which doesn't seem elegant. Let's fix that by creating a class for the Car object and then use it to simply add the attributes directly.

Start by selecting File ➤ New ➤ File... and then choosing Core Data from the left pane and the NSManagedObject subclass on the right (Figure 21-14). Then press Next and you will see the screen in Figure 21-15

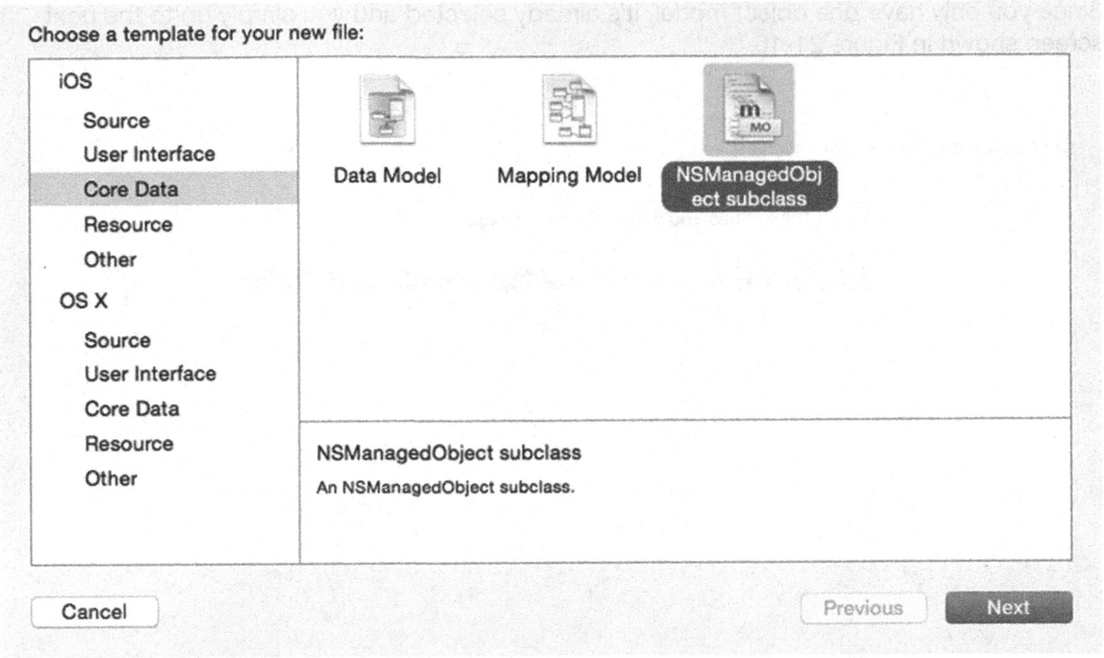

Figure 21-14. Creating Car Entity

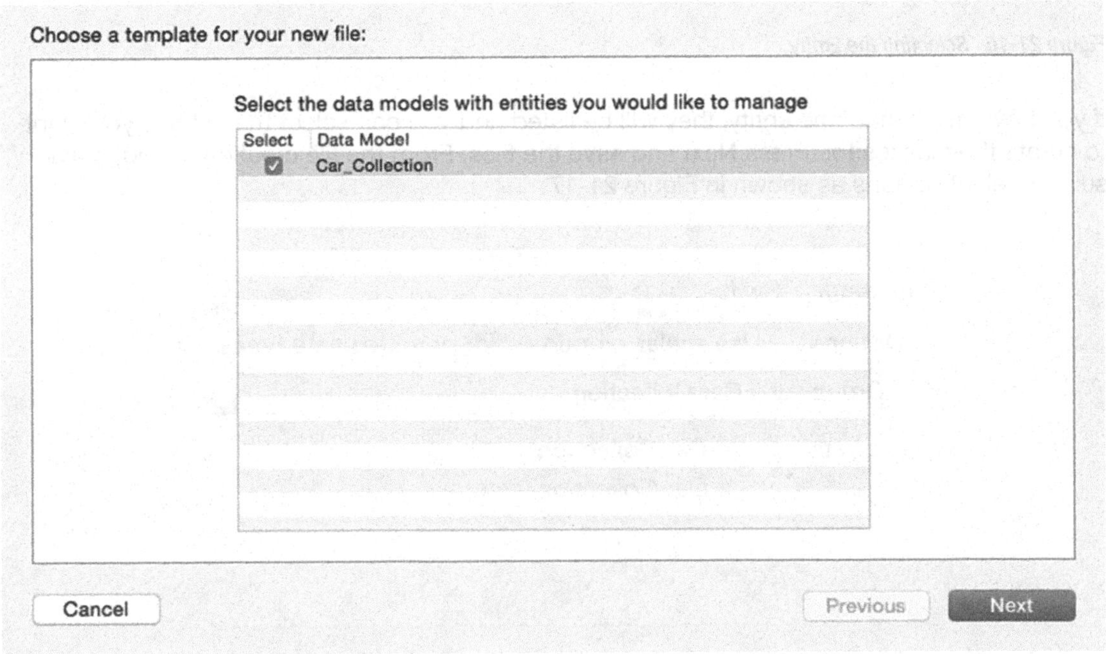

Figure 21-15. Selecting the Object Model

Since you only have one object model, it's already selected and you simply go to the next screen shown in Figure 21-16

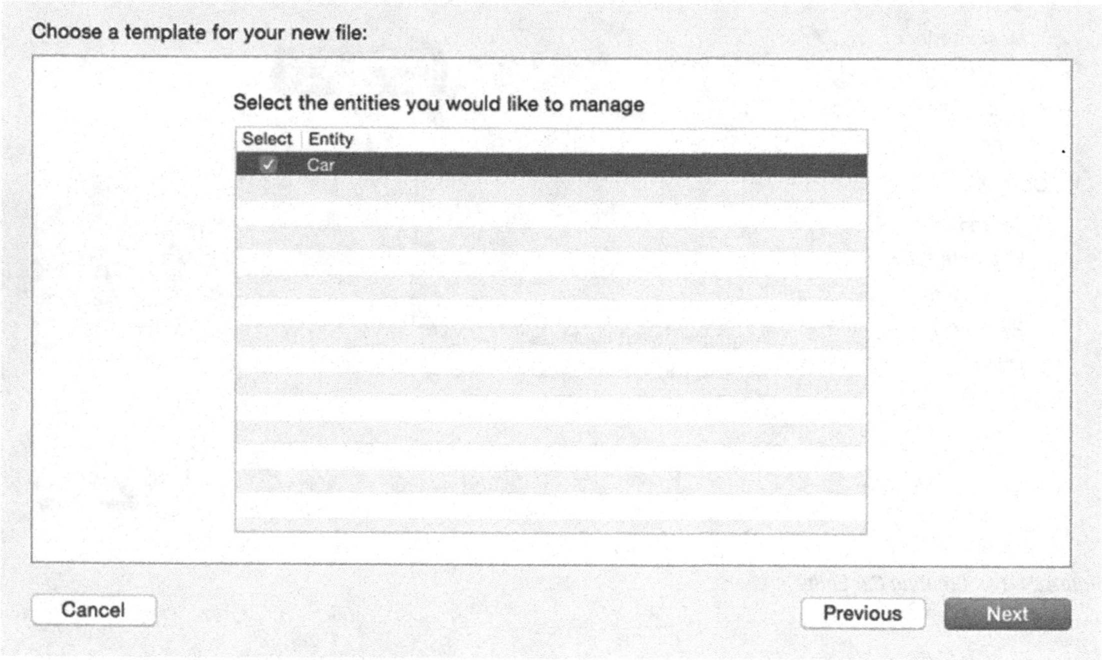

Figure 21-16. Selecting the Entity

If you have more than one entity, they will be listed and you can select the entities you want to create the classes for. Press Next and save the files. From the file creation dialog, make sure to select options as shown in Figure 21-17.

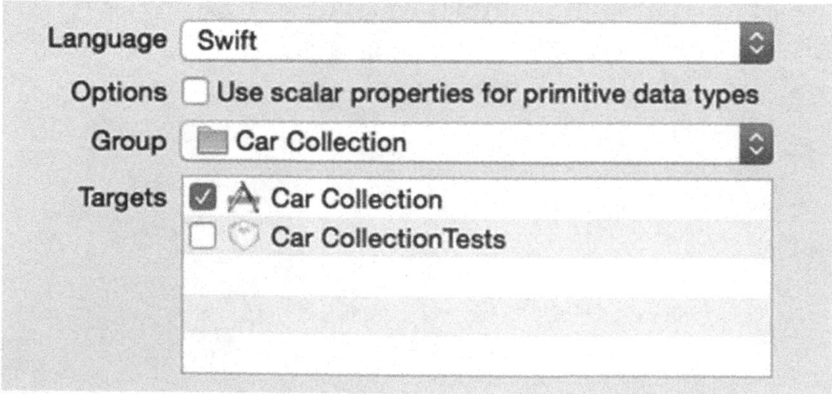

Figure 21-17. File Creation Options

Now you have a class called Car:

```
class Car: NSManagedObject {
    @NSManaged var color: String
    @NSManaged var doors: NSNumber
    @NSManaged var make: String
    @NSManaged var model: String
    @NSManaged var year: NSDate
}
```

The properties are marked with @NSManaged, which tells Swift that these properties need special treatment when they're accessed. If you try build and run, you'll get a warning from Core Data that it can't find the class for the entity:

```
2015-02-07 22:26:06.394 Car Collection[17018:3500332] CoreData: warning: Unable to load
class named 'Car' for entity 'Car'.  Class not found, using default NSManagedObject instead.
```

What's happening here? Well, remember that Swift uses namespaces. The actual name of the class is `Car_Collection.Car`, which is indeed not the class `Car` Core Data is looking for. As you learned in Chapter 18, you have to give this class an Objective-C name that Core Data can understand. Just add `@objc(Car)` before the `class` keyword. Now update the rest of the methods to use this new class.

The save method in the editor view controller now looks much better:

```
@IBAction func save(sender: UIBarButtonItem) {
    let context = self.managedObjectContext
    let entityName = "Car"
    let newCar = NSEntityDescription.insertNewObjectForEntityForName(entityName,
    inManagedObjectContext: context!) as Car
    newCar.make = self.makeTextField.text ?? "Unknown Make"
    newCar.model = self.modelTextField.text ?? "Unknown Model"
    newCar.color = self.colorTextField.text ?? "Unknown Color"
    let doors : NSString = self.numberOfDoorsTextField.text ?? "2"
    let number = NSNumber(int: doors.intValue)
    newCar.doors = number
    newCar.year = self.makeYearDatePicker.date

    var error: NSError? = nil
    if !context!.save(&error) {
    }

    self.presentingViewController?.dismissViewControllerAnimated(true, completion: nil)
}
```

Now update the `MasterViewController` to use this new class to configure the cell.

```
func configureCell(cell: UITableViewCell, atIndexPath indexPath: NSIndexPath) {
    let car = self.fetchedResultsController.objectAtIndexPath(indexPath) as Car
    cell.textLabel!.text = car.model
}
```

Now you can use the properties of the entity directly instead of using the `objectForKey`, and casting the correct type.

Summary

Core Data is a small framework but requires some time and effort to learn and to understand its idiosyncrasies. Many books have been written on the subject. One such book is *Pro Core Data for iOS* (Apress, 2011). This chapter is just a taste of what Core Data can and can't do. You have to look at the life cycle of objects and different parts of the systems and see what roles they play. There are many libraries that make working with Core Data much easier and handle most of the boilerplate code.

Chapter 22

Consuming RESTful Services

If you have a Twitter account or a Facebook account, when you use their mobile applications you are consuming their services via a REST API.

Representational State Transfer (REST) defines an architecture, not a protocol, for designing Web services that consume system resources. It defines how the resource states are accessed and transferred over HTTP.

The key features of REST Web services are:

- They use HTTP methods only.
- They are stateless.
- Endpoints are defined as directory structures.
- Data is transferred using XML, JSON or both.

HTTP Methods

There are four HTTP methods we will be using today, GET, PUT, POST and DELETE. These methods are defined by the HTTP protocol. There are other methods but we will not disucss those

- GET is used to retrieve a resource from the server.
- POST is used to create a resource on the server.
- PUT is used to modify an existing resource on the server.
- DELETE is used to remove a resource from the server.

It's not good design to use a specific method for the purpose of other method. For instance, it's not a good idea to use GET to create a resource on the server.

Being Stateless

Since REST services need to scale and serve lots of requests, it's difficult to keep track of each connection between multiple requests from the same client. This is especially true in an environment where the backend may use load balancers, proxies, or failovers. So every call must be completely independent of every other call, and must send all the information needed to complete the request.

Endpoints

Each endpoint must be defined as a path to a resource; resources are also known as URIs. When designing the endpoints, make sure they are well thought out and extensible. Here are some examples:

```
GET http://www.mydomain.com/v1/user/<userId>
GET http://www.mydomain.com/v1/forum/rooms
GET http://www.mydomain.com/v1/forum/topic/<topidId>
POST http://www.mydomain.com/v1/forum/topic/<topicId>
```

Data Formats

When sending the retrieving resource, it can be packaged in a structured format that the server and client know how to interpret. The officially recommended formats are either XML (eXtensible Markup Language) or JSON (JavaScript Object Notation). Apple provides built-in APIs to decode and encode into these formats. Depending on which format you end up using, make sure to set the correct HTTP headers to indicate what kind of data it is (Table 22-1).

Table 22-1.* *Recommended formats

MIME type	Content Type
JSON	application/json
XML	application/xml

Network Access

iOS and OSX provide an extensive set of APIs to handle these requests. Some of the APIs you'll be using are:

- NSURL and NSURLComponents, which allow you to create the URIs for the endpoints.
- NSURLRequest, along with URL and other information, makes a complete request needed to interact with sever
- NSURLSession is the actual object that uses the request to download and upload the resource

- NSJSONSerialization encodes and decodes JSON objects for transfer
- NSXMLParser decodes XML data.

Now that you have most of the pieces, it's time to create the application to put the pieces together. There are many APIs to choose from for your REST application. I'm going to work with the Hacker News API.

> **Note** Hacker News is social news site that has stories related to programmers. You'll find the official API at `https://github.com/HackerNews/API`.

The application will download the top stories and display them in a table view. First let's take a look at the API. The base URL for the app to make calls to the API is:

```
https://hacker-news.firebaseio.com/v0/
```

And some of the endpoints we are interested in are:

`/topstories.json` returns the current set of top stories on the front page, returning the identifiers for the stories as an array.

```
[identifier1, identifier2, ... ]
```

`/item/<itemnumber>.json` returns the detail information about one of the stories. You specify the story identifier you need more information about, such as `/item/<identifier>.json` and the typical result will be returned as key-value pairs (that is, a dictionary), as shown in Table 22-2.

Table 22-2. Key-value pairs

Key	Value
Id	Unique identifier for the item
By	User who posted the item
type	One of job, story, comment, poll, or pollopt
time	Time item was created on the system
title	Title of the item
url	URL of the item, if any
score	Current score of the item
kids	An array of comment identifiers

There are a few others, but I'll focus on these for now. Let's create a new project and call it News. I'm going to use project template called Master-Detail Application, as shown in Figure 22-1.

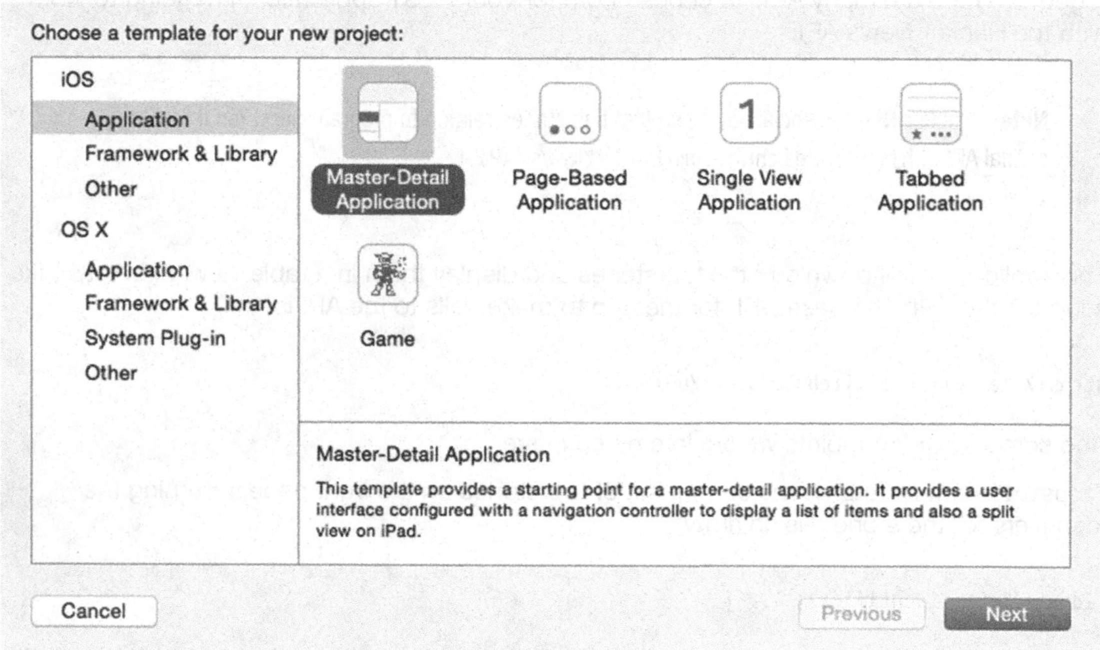

***Figure 22-1.** Choosing the Master-Detail Application template*

First we need to create a class that represents an item, so we will create a new Swift file using the Swift file template from the new file panel. The file is called `Item.swift` and it defines some properties and a method to update the properties:

```
public class Item {
    let identifier : Int

    init(dictionary : [String : AnyObject]) {
        let identifier = dictionary["id"] as NSNumber
        self.identifier = Int(identifier.intValue)
        self.score = 0
        self.update(dictionary)
    }

    var type : String? = nil
    var by : String? = nil
    var date : NSDate? = nil
    var title : String? = nil
    var url : NSURL? = nil
    var score : Int32
    var text : String? = nil
```

```
    public func update(dictionary : [String : AnyObject]) {
        self.type = dictionary["type"] as? String
        self.by = dictionary["by"] as? String

        let unixTime = dictionary["time"] as? NSNumber
        if let time : NSNumber = unixTime {
            self.date = NSDate(timeIntervalSince1970 : time.doubleValue) as NSDate
        }
        self.title = dictionary["title"] as? String

        let urlString = dictionary["url"] as? String
        if let string = urlString {
            self.url = NSURL(string: string)
        }
        let score = dictionary["score"] as? NSNumber

        if let value : NSNumber = score {
            self.score = Int32(value.intValue)
        }
        self.text = dictionary["text"] as? String
    }
}
```

Next we need to connect to the service and download items. We will download the identifiers for the top stories and then, for each of these stories, we will download the details.

In the MasterViewController we will create a couple of functions that will download the items I need.

```
    private func  getTopStories() -> Void {
        let url = NSURL(string: NetworkManagerBaseURL + "/v0/topstories.json")
        var urlRequest = NSMutableURLRequest(URL: url!)
        urlRequest.HTTPMethod = "GET"
      NSURLConnection.sendAsynchronousRequest(urlRequest, queue: self.operationQueue)
      {[unowned self] (response, responseData, error) -> Void in
            if let data = responseData {

 let objects = NSJSONSerialization.JSONObjectWithData(data, options:
 NSJSONReadingOptions(0), error: nil) as? NSArray

                self.downloadStoriesInformation(objects!)
            }
        }
    }
```

First we will create a URL for the endpoint by creating an NSURL object. Once we have the URL object we then create a request from that URL. After we have the request object, we want to set the method we will use for downloading. In this case we want GET.

> **Note** GET is the default method NSURLRequest uses if you don't change it. We will set it to be verbose.

Next we use the NSURLConnection class method to download the data. This method returns an HTTP response object, and data if there is data, or an error if there was an error.

We can't use the raw NSData so we have to convert the data into a proper native object. We do this using NSJSONSerialization. After We have the top stories we need to download each story detail.

We are going to set up the few items we will need before starting to code. The first item is the base URL from which we will download the news articles:

```
let NetworkManagerBaseURL = "http://hacker-news.firebaseio.com"
```

Next we need an operation queue where I'll schedule the download processes.

```
var operationQueue : NSOperationQueue = {
    var operationQueue = NSOperationQueue()
    operationQueue.name = "com.apress.DownloadQueue"
    operationQueue.maxConcurrentOperationCount = 1
    return operationQueue
}()
```

The next method downloads the story details for each story, and once we have all the stories we show them in my tableview.

```
private func downloadStoriesInformation (storyIdentifiers : NSArray) -> Void {
    var downloaded : Int = 0
    let count = storyIdentifiers.count
    for var index : Int = 0; index < count; index++ {
        let storyIdentifier = storyIdentifiers[index] as NSNumber
        let urlString = NetworkManagerBaseURL + "/v0/item/" + storyIdentifier.stringValue + ".json"
        let url = NSURL(string: urlString)
        var urlRequest = NSMutableURLRequest(URL: url!)
        urlRequest.HTTPMethod = "GET"

NSURLConnection.sendAsynchronousRequest(urlRequest, queue: self.operationQueue) {[unowned
self] (response, responseData, error) -> Void in
            if let data = responseData {
                let object = NSJSONSerialization.JSONObjectWithData(data, options:
                NSJSONReadingOptions(0), error: nil) as? NSDictionary
                let item = Item(dictionary: object as [String : AnyObject])
                self.stories.setObject(item, forKey: storyIdentifier)
                downloaded++
                if downloaded == count {
                    self.objects.removeAllObjects()
                    self.objects.addObjectsFromArray(storyIdentifiers)
                    dispatch_async(dispatch_get_main_queue()) { [unowned self] in
                        self.tableView.reloadData()
                    }
                }
            }
        }
    }
}
```

After we have the data, we want to display it. To do this weneed to modify the `cellForRow:atIndexPath:` method to display the title of the story.

```
override func tableView(tableView: UITableView, cellForRowAtIndexPath indexPath:
NSIndexPath) -> UITableViewCell {
    let cell = tableView.dequeueReusableCellWithIdentifier("Cell", forIndexPath: indexPath)
    as UITableViewCell

    let object = objects[indexPath.row] as NSNumber
    let item = self.stories[object] as Item
    cell.textLabel!.text = item.title
    return cell
}
```

We have the order of the stories in the `objects` property, as well as the data related to how to get the stories.

Once we have the list of stories and titles, to actually read the article we will use the SFSafariViewController, add the import SafarServices at the top of the file, and then we update the tableview didSelectItem method

```
override func tableView(tableView: UITableView, didSelectRowAtIndexPath indexPath:
NSIndexPath) {
    if let object = objects[indexPath.row] as? NSNumber, item = stories[object] as? Item,
    url = item.url {
        let safariViewController = SFSafariViewController.init(URL: url)
        self.navigationController?.pushViewController(safariViewController, animated: true)
    }
    tableView.deselectRowAtIndexPath(indexPath, animated: true)
}
```

Security

Starting with iOS 9, Apple has disabled for applications to connect with non encrypted http servers, if you try to run the application you will not see any data and if you were looking at the console output you will get this message:

```
2015-11-02 00:19:09.762 News[12329:2138511] App Transport Security has blocked a cleartext
HTTP (http://) resource load since it is insecure. Temporary exceptions can be configured
via your app's Info.plist file.
```

Since our application sever endpoint is not encrypted we have to tell the Transport Security that we really want to talk to our server unencrypted. Also since this app will show links from other website potentially non-encrypted. We will just allow our app to have connected to any server encrypted or not encrypted.

> **Note** this is a not a good security policy, can lead to compromised system, so it is recommended that you use this option very carfully.

You need to add an option to the Info.plist file select the info.plist file and add value of key `NSAppTransportSecurity` or in pretty version `App Transport Security Settings` make sure the type is Dictionary.

Next we need to add a subvalue with key `NSAllowsArbitraryLoads` or pretty version Allow Arbitrary Loads, make sure this value is of type Bool and the value is set to true. Build and run and there you are.

▶ Status bar tinting parameters	Dictionary	(1 item)
▶ Supported interface orientations	Array	(3 items)
▼ App Transport Security Settings	Dictionary	(1 item)
Allow Arbitrary Loads	Boolean	YES

Summary

This is a quick look at REST services, what they are and how you can use them to access the data from servers. This is the same method a Twitter client would use to connect to its server and download tweets. If you do a quick search on the web for REST API, you'll find many companies that offer REST APIs for their resources. If you plan on writing a client-server application for mobile, this a good solution.

Index

D

E

M

N

O

P, Q

R

S